Human Services Today

Human Services Today

Karin Eriksen

Reston Publishing Company, Inc., Reston, Virginia
A Prentice-Hall Company

Library of Congress Cataloging in Publication Data

Eriksen, Karin.
   Human services today.

   Includes bibliographies and index.
   1.   Social service—United States.   2.   United
States—Social policy.   3.   Helping behavior.
I.   Title.
HV95.E75   362'.973   76-47448
ISBN 0-87909-336-6

© 1977 by
Reston Publishing Company, Inc.
A Prentice-Hall Company
Reston, Virginia 22090

10   9   8   7   6   5   4   3   2

For Barbara Bennett Blum,

a very special human services leader

Acknowledgements

Gratitude and sincere thanks are in order to many people for helping me with planning and completing this book:

to my students and colleagues at Staten Island Community College for their inspiration and encouragement

to Audrey Cohen, Alan Gartner, and Leonard Romney—three outstanding human services educators—for their guidance and insights

to my family and friends—especially Ricia Marra, Jane Goldman, and Valerie Roth—for their confidence in me and their support

to the many people it has been my privilege to work with and, hopefully, to help during my career in human services

Contents

Preface   ix

chapter one
An Overview of Human Services   1

    Contemporary Society, 3; Traditional Service Patterns, 6; The Whole Person, 7; Human Services, 8; The Service Bridge, 10; An Interdisciplinary Approach, 13.

chapter two
A History of Human Services   21

    Building the Human Services Bridge, 24; Early History, 26.

chapter three
Human Services Today   47

    Turn of the Century, 49; Emerging Human Services Thinking, 51; Mid-Century, 58; Today and Tomorrow, 63.

chapter four
Social Policy and Planning   67

    What is Social Policy?, 69; Human Services Policy, 73; Social Planning for Human Services, 75; Research in the Human Services, 80; Human Services Modules, 81.

chapter five
Use of Self   87

Tool of the Trade, 89; Components of a Helping Relationship, 96.

chapter six
Understanding People   101

Base of Understanding, 103; Biological Considerations, 107;
Cultural Considerations, 110; Psychological Considerations,
114; People with Problems, 121; Unfinished Business, 122.

chapter seven
Working With People   125

What is a Helping Person?, 128; The Helping Process, 130.

chapter eight
Working With Systems   145

Social Systems, 147; Working with Groups, 148; Systems
Skills, 156; A Word on Change, 164.

chapter nine
Social Problems   167

The Emperor's New Clothes, 169; Blaming the Victim, 171;
Warehousing and Other Band-Aids, 175; Family Fade-Out,
178; Social Solutions, 181.

chapter ten
Trends and Issues in Human Services   185

New Priorities—New Directions, 188; No Time for Amateurs, 190; Everybody's Ball Game, 191; A Commitment to
Windmills, 193.

Index   195

Preface

The emergence of Human Services as a perspective and as a profession is an expression both of contemporary human need and of current societal response to need. Essentially, human services is a new answer to a serious rethinking of the ever-present question: *What is helpful?*

Human Services Today attempts to answer that question for the reader by reviewing salient past and present efforts at helpfulness and by suggesting some values, attitudes, and skills which are fundamental to helpfulness. The book begins with an assumption that many of the systems designed to serve people are decidedly *un*helpful and moves on to look at ways in which systems can become more responsive to human need and, consequently, more helpful to people and to society.

At the outset, it is just as well that I openly acknowledge that *Human Services Today* is not a traditional textbook with a purely objective presentation of data and developments. On the contrary, by design, the overview and review of human services presented here is sometimes irreverent and often subjective. This approach was chosen for two reasons. First, it seems to me that a much-needed *re*humanizing of services cannot occur if we, in every branch of human services, do not soon stop hiding and overcome our professional distance from each other and from those we try to serve. We all have to look more closely at what we are doing and why we are doing it that particular way. We need to ask "Why?" a lot more than we do, if we are to be truly helpful as professionals and as a profession. This is no time for resting on our professional laurels. Second, we need to encourage new professionals entering the field to also ask "Why?". It has been my experience in teaching students of human services that their ability to be really helpful is hinged as much on their solid understanding of themselves and the world around them as on the mastery of a set of skills and techniques. None of us has all the answers, but it is vitally important that we keep asking the questions—of ourselves and of each other.

One little book, no matter how ambitious its author, could presume to be a definitive work on the expansive and expanding field that is human services today. There will be, therefore, some things left unsaid and other things hardly noted in this book. That is probably just as well. In a sense, every book should be only an introduction; an invitation to further exploration by the reader on his own initiative. *Human Services Today* is such a beginning, I hope. It is also my hope that it will lend some perspective and stimulate an openness to new ideas in the student which will enhance his or her commitment to the improvement of human services for the benefit of all of us.

History has confirmed the truth of the adage, "The more you know, the more you don't know"! In human services, this will probably always be true. There will always be more to know about human beings and more to learn about the ways to serve them best.

Although I certainly would not be pleased if, when you finish this book, you know less about human services than you did when you started reading, I do hope that *Human Services Today* spurs you on to learn more about people and their systems—from other books and classes and from living.

KARIN ERIKSEN

chapter one

An Overview of Human Services

Human Services: What is it? How did it develop? Where is it going? It is the author's intent to trace the historical roots of human services; to summarize its present philosophical base; to describe its practical applications; to assess its current place in American history; and to observe the trends and issues which will direct its future growth.

CONTEMPORARY SOCIETY

Human Services is a new profession, emerging full force in 1970s America. It is essentially the child of a society in transition. America has come a long way in two hundred years and during that time enormous changes have taken place in our way of life. In no other time in history has so much changed so fast. Twentieth century America has been heir to so much rapid technological growth and social change that people have been left more than a little dizzy from the enormity of it all.

Since 1900, modern technology has created many of the every-day things most of us take for granted now: automobiles, airplanes, electricity, telephones, air conditioning, television, synthetic fabrics, frozen foods and refrigerators, nuclear and solar energy, and count-less medical and other advances to make life longer and healthier. For the first time in history, we are within sight of an era when people will no longer have to do back-breaking labor in order to survive. Clearly, all of these advancements could be cause for celebration. Most people are now living more comfortably than ever before and have more conveniences and more free time to use as they please. Why is no one cheering?

People aren't cheering because somewhere during our society's gallop into the future, life became very complicated and people be-

3

came uncomfortable in their own world. Ours is called a **Transitional Age** because society's old ways and old values don't seem to fit or make as much sense anymore. At the same time, the new ways and new values aren't yet very stable or satisfying for most people.

During this country's first two hundred years, Americans were guided by a system of traditions and beliefs that cohesively defined and directed people's attitudes about life and about themselves, and made sense of the social order in most people's minds. Americans derived their greatest strength from their families, their religions, and their communities. Life was comparatively simple. People tended to stay put—in their work, in their towns and neighborhoods, and in their thinking. They believed in the democratic ideals of "life, liberty, and the pursuit of happiness" and dreamed the American Dream—that hard work and persistence would be rewarded by wealth and success (i.e., "Anyone can be president"). There were, after all, incredible natural resources in this young country and frontiers waiting to be conquered. People from all over the world immigrated to the Land of Equal Opportunity with its promise of a better life.

And life did get better for almost everyone. But, there were significant drawbacks to the achievements of industrialization and advancing technology. Millions of Americans worked as hard as they possibly could and never achieved anything close to great wealth or success. It began to look as if the American Dream was more wishful thinking than attainable reality. It began to appear that machines, not people, held the key to success. As people became more and more dependent on their machines, the fabric of society changed drastically. Farmers left their roots and moved to the cities to be closer to both the production and consumption of the vast goods that the American market place had become capable of offering. Traditional supports, such as the extended family and the church, lost much of their significance and influence over people's lives. The average person became impatient with "the good old days" and turned his hopes toward the future in which everyone seemed to have unlimited potential for a better life.

It's probably a fact of human nature that "the more people get, the more they want." Some call this the Revolution of Rising Expectations. There's nothing inherently wrong with wanting more—the problem arises when "having more" becomes an end in itself. When people began to determine their own worth (as well as other people's) by their buying power and to look for satisfaction from things instead of from other people, it should have been clear that our values were being turned upside down. "Keeping up with the Joneses," which is now so characteristic of American life and the relentless pursuit of "things" which keeping up requires, has taken its toll on life, liberty, and the pursuit of happiness.

Contemporary society, with its emphasis on competition, acquisition, and materialism, has not made people comfortable in their modernized world. People seem to be unsure of where they're headed these days or even of who they are. The prescription to "do your own thing" hasn't proven to be a useful antidote to the uneasiness of modern times. We've been called "hollow" and "plastic" people—isolated, bored, cynical, lonely, and insecure—dwarfed by our own technology. Many, many Americans feel unimportant and useless—uncommitted and without a sense of purpose; doing work (if they can find any) that is monotonous and meaningless for them; feeling overwhelmed instead of enriched by the incredible changes of modern life.

If people aren't entirely satisfied with themselves, they are even less pleased or optimistic about the larger society. We're just beginning to recover from one of the most shocking periods in our political history. The signs of the times look awfully grim: poverty in plenty, pollution, corruption, skyrocketing unemployment, energy shortages, a credibility gap, violence in the streets, a "generation gap" at home, colliding values, fading traditions, and market place mentalities. An undercurrent of futility exists and a sense that something very important is missing in our life and times.

Americans have been caught off guard and caught up in a whirlwind of social and economic growth and change that happened too fast. Neither we as individuals nor as a society were prepared for all the consequences and side effects of so much rapid, decisive change. Obviously our technology didn't bring the Utopia so many anticipated. But, it isn't exactly Doomsday, either! It's *our* technology, after all, and we can do with it what we will! And, we will.

Right now we need a chance to catch up with ourselves—a time for getting our priorities in order. Our present fears and conflicts, our confusion and disillusionment may actually be serving a useful purpose. Conflict and stress are essential ingredients for growth. With all the conflict and stress surrounding us these days, chances are very good that our society will grow in a healthier direction now. Life doesn't have to be mechanical and people don't have to be compartmentalized.

There are already many encouraging indications that America is beginning to settle down and sort things out and develop a new and durable set of people-centered values. One of the outstanding examples of our society's intention to chart a new course which gives prominence to personal, not technological, values is the recent creation and blossoming of the human services profession.

TRADITIONAL SERVICE PATTERNS

Our society's capacity to help people has mushroomed right along with our technology. Most of the comprehensive social welfare measures we all enjoy today are twentieth century inventions: social security, income maintenance, workmen's compensation, unemployment insurance, public education, Medicare, the minimum wage and even income tax, numerous other programs, services, and social utilities. All have been designed and supported by society to sustain and enhance the quality of life for every American. People are now eligible for more of society's benefits than their counterparts in earlier ages would ever have anticipated. But, people aren't necessarily cheering about all this either.

Although society is now taking significantly increased responsibility for meeting people's needs, our traditional patterns of delivering services have not proven to be entirely adequate to the task. Just as technology has been a mixed blessing, so have our helping efforts. The "Golden Rule" is still very much an American belief, but today we often don't know who our neighbors are, and when we do, the traditional, informal helping hand is usually not enough to help them meet their needs. Enter the Bureaucracy—a twentieth century invention we could probably do nicely without! In every area where society has made organized efforts to meet people's needs—such as health, education, law, welfare—a bureaucracy has sprung up to administer those programs and services. In many respects, each bureaucracy is a microcosm of our larger societal problems. It is often impersonal, dehumanizing, and alienating; likely to be inefficient and inadequate; and sometimes even downright irrelevant or destructive to meeting people's needs. The very complexity of our service machinery and organizations has only diluted their usefulness to people. As each bureaucracy develops, it tends to become more complex, more interested in maintaining its own status quo, and reciprocally less concerned with people than with procedures. It is not uncommon to hear horror stories of people's needs and problems being buried and unresolved by a harrassed clerk or incompetent computer at some mysterious point in a bureaucratic structure.

 A technological society prizes specialization of function to increase productivity and efficiency. That may work with machines, but it doesn't always work very well with people. Yet, as helping was "industrialized" the importance of specializing got high priority and the concept of comprehensiveness in service delivery necessarily had to take a back seat. Also, like the market place, competition entered into helping. It seems almost laughable that each service profession should become concerned with empire-building and fighting over the size of their turf in the realm of service delivery. But, that's precisely what's been happening, to an alarming extent. With all these business-like frictions and priorities, it is no small wonder that people aren't cheering about the quality of present-day service delivery. As each service system has become more bureaucratized, more specialized, more fragmented, and more separated from other systems, its responsiveness to people and their needs has considerably diminished.

THE WHOLE PERSON

Worst of all, as services have become excessively compartmentalized, there has been a growing tendency to compartmentalize people, as well! It isn't easy anymore to find a service system which is able to address the needs of a *whole person.* For example, If you need a job, go to one bureaucracy. . . . If you don't feel well, go to another. . . . If your child can't read, go someplace else. . . . If you need money, try another office . . . and so on. Is that really helpful? If it's frustrating to read about the wastes of manpower and helping resources, imagine how it must feel to have to ask for help. Even rats don't like their mazes. Why should we?

Knowing the Whole Person

There is a well-known fable about some ancient wise men who each had a viewpoint based on a rather limited perspective of a particular situation. The men, who were blind, were positioned at different parts of an elephant. Then they were asked to describe what they thought they were touching and experiencing. Predictably, their stories were each very different. A tusk is, after all, quite different from a tail. The funny thing was that each man was certain that he was knowledgeably describing an entity, not just a part of a far more significant whole. Therein lies the problem with traditional service delivery channels. Each service channel only "sees" a part of the person and, therefore, usually doesn't "see" the whole person at all.

It goes without saying that it's more important to understand people than elephants. But, our service structures are falling short of the mark. Something more is needed to insure services which will be delivered effectively and efficiently while also being comprehensive enough to meet the needs of the whole person. There is a growing awareness that change is needed for serving people and for the many professions engaged in serving people. A better mesh of meeting people's individual needs and serving the public interest is already beginning to occur within our service systems. This new and promising change is called human services.

HUMAN SERVICES

What exactly *is* human services? Defining that term has proven to be perhaps the most difficult and most crucial task in writing this book. When I asked my colleagues for their thoughts on a definition, they laughingly replied, "Services to humans, of course." After a lengthy search through the literature, much gnashing of teeth, and many attempts at a more scholarly explanation, I've come to the conclusion that they were absolutely right. In its broadest sense, a human service is going on whenever one person is employed to be of service to another.

Human services is the unifying and integrating profession of our society's many social welfare subsystems—health, education, mental health, welfare, family services, corrections, child care, vocational rehabilitation, housing, community service, and the law. There are now over 2,000 careers within the field of human services, making it a major American industry. In the United States today, far more people are now employed in the provision of services than in the production of goods. Every year, increasing numbers of people are involved in

HUMAN SERVICES SUB-SYSTEMS

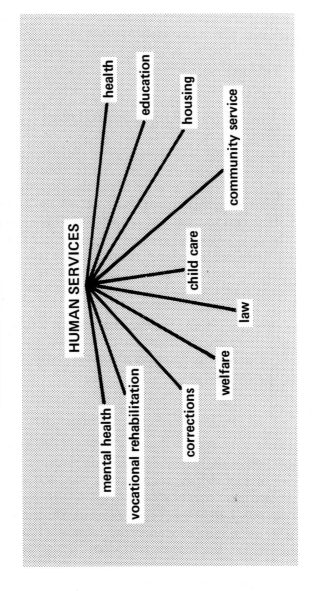

HUMAN SERVICES

health
education
housing
community service
child care
law
welfare
corrections
vocational rehabilitation
mental health

both the delivery and the consumption of human services. That the field of human services is growing so rapidly and steadily is a very reassuring sign of our society's renewed emphasis on the importance of helping people. It is also a clear indication that traditional service systems are going to be improved, expanded, and integrated in order to serve people better.

THE SERVICE BRIDGE

Human services is often called the "umbrella" for our society's subsystems which are involved either directly or indirectly in promoting and reinforcing satisfying, healthy living and community cohesiveness. While this comparison may be useful, human services could more accurately be described as *a bridge between people and systems.* It is the profession charged with the responsibility to close the gap between traditional service systems and the needs and rights of the whole person. Human services has taken up the challenge to serve the whole person—and to make society more whole in the process.

As in every profession, human services has a cohesive underlying philosophy and ethic; a range of clearly defined tasks and goals; a specific body of knowledge; a unique set of skills; and a career ladder for its professionals.

The Human Services Philosophy

Human services reflects the values and priorities of American society. Its philosophy also embodies the diversity of interests, needs, values, and lifestyles of a pluralistic nation with over 200,000,000 citizens. Human services is an organized service effort to put the ideals of a democratic society into action. The following Human Service Principles represent the philosophy and ethics that are fundamental to not only human services but to our democratic way of life as well.

I.   Human services is the embodiment of our national commitment to building a just society based on respect for people's rights and needs. Human services isn't taking a philosophical backseat to ponder, "Who is 'sick'—society or the individual?", but is committed to an action-oriented approach to services.

The affirmation of our country's civil rights legislation guarantees people the right to privacy, confidentiality, services and equity. No longer are human services to be considered a privilege; they are the right of every American citizen. As further confirmation of a belief in equal rights, human services is committed to the conviction that services should be equally accessible, and of the same good quality for all people. We do not believe that some people are more "equal" than others and we, therefore, will strive for a just distribution of services and resources among people.

II.   Every individual in our society is entitled to services which will prevent his pain, maintain his integrity, enable him to deal with his realities, stimulate his personal growth, and promote a satisfying life for him and his family. To these ends, human services should be utilized to diminish each individual's vulnerability to the environment. Also, since most people's problems are externally caused, those forces in society which interfere with the provision of human services for people's needs will become the target of change and alteration. Human services endeavors to make systems flexible enough to serve people. Service subsystems will need to give significantly higher priority to people than to organizational concerns.

The whole person should be served by human services. People should not be known by their labels. No one is only a toothache, a neurotic, or a learning disability. The provision of human services needs to be undertaken in an atmosphere of respect and understanding of every individual's uniqueness, with full recognition that people are dynamic, constantly changing in an ongoing process of "becoming."

III.   Prevention of people's problems and discomforts is as important a part of human services as restitution and rehabilitation after the fact. Human services has a commitment to assessing the quality of life available to people and to anticipating any threats which may arise in society to disable people and/or deprive them of their rights.

IV.   The integration of human services is crucial to their effectiveness. Human services is engaged in maintaining open channels of communication between its subsystems in order to rapidly mobilize them on the whole person's behalf. If human services are to be appropriate, adequate, and relevant to meeting people's needs, they must be comprehensive in nature. Linkages must be established between subsystems to insure that a network of human services is readily available for those who need these services. The ideal human service network will ultimately exclude no one. Increased knowledge and technological innovations will be utilized as integrative mechanisms to insure optimally effective services and to maximize society's resources for its people.

V. *Human services are accountable to the consumers.* The people who consume human services have the right to participate in services as they choose and if they choose. Human services is service between equals. The consumers of services also have the right to an active role in the evaluation and planning of services intended for their utilization. No aspect of human services should be hidden from consumer awareness or impervious to consumer control. The core of human services is its commitment to bridging the gap between consumers and services. To that end, consumer participation should be actively encouraged in all areas of service delivery.

Human Services Tasks and Goals

The paramount goal of human services is to enable people to live more satisfying, more autonomous, and more productive lives, through the utilization of society's knowledge, resources, and technological innovations. To that end, society's systems will be working for its people.

A respected colleague of mine has hung a sign over his desk that reads:

PEOPLE BEFORE PAPER

This is the essence of human services. Every subsystem within the human services profession shares this commitment and undertakes those chores specific to its system in the context of this paramount goal: bringing the best quality service to people as quickly and effectively as possible. This comprehensive here-and-now approach to problem-solving is shared by every branch of human services.

Given the enormous scope of the human services profession and the global nature of its goals, it becomes evident that the tasks required to achieve them will necessarily be challenging, difficult, innovative, and extensive. There will undoubtedly be as many tasks as there are problems and people needing services.

It is the exception, not the rule, that a problem leading someone to human services will be "simple" and resolved in a "one-shot" encounter. It is much more typical for an individual to be confronted with a number of related difficulties. Problems seem to run in packs, more often than not. Because people and their problems are usually complicated, the delivery of services often is, as well. One of the frequent tasks of human services is to *un*complicate the service delivery process. For example, Mrs. Jones may be told by her doctor that if she is to get over her lingering illness, she will need better nutrition, adequate housing, and some relief from her full-time child-caring duties so that she can rest. Obviously neither Mrs. Jones nor her doctor alone can bring about the delivery of all the services she needs. They must be secured through the coordinated involvement of several subsystems of human services, i.e., housing, welfare, and day care.

AN INTERDISCIPLINARY
APPROACH

Integral to effective service delivery for Mrs. Jones and everyone else is use of an *interdisciplinary approach* to helping. The old saying that "Two heads are better than one" is very true in human services. The "heads" from the disciplines (or subsystems) that make up human services often need to work closely together to achieve their common goal. This is how a network of services is established and maintained. People have to talk to each other and cross the boundaries of their particular fields within human services. To stimulate this exchange between subsystems is another important task of human services. Traditional service patterns have been quite similar to parallel railroad tracks, making integration of services very difficult, if not impossible. Human services is an effort to make those tracks converge so that service comprehensiveness is possible.

Human services is also a catalyst for change—for people and for systems. In addition to linking systems and bringing them closer to people, human services has still another task: to stimulate change within its own subsystems and in larger society when such change would significantly benefit people. To accomplish this goal, human services must take on the task of evaluating its own effectiveness in a continuing commitment to improving service delivery and thereby enhancing people's lives. Traditional service patterns have become inadequate because they neglect to "see the forest for the trees." If human services is to benefit from history, it must maintain an alert interest in systematically monitoring and evaluating itself and stimulating changes wherever they are indicated to remove any barrier between people and adequate, appropriate services. Its efforts in this direction will be guided by the assumption that if things are not working out well, we may need to change the systems, *not* the people. The greatest strength of human services is making systems fit people. Attending to this task will insure its future effectiveness.

Every task and goal within human services is undertaken to put the profession's principles into affirmative action. All the strategies developed within and throughout human services will be based on its commitment to enriching people's lives.

Human Services Knowledge

Because human services is greater than the sum of all its parts, its body of knowledge has incorporated information from each of its subsystems—and then some! Now that doesn't mean that everyone in human services must know all about medicine, mental health, teaching, or law enforcement. Yet, there is a core of knowledge that is shared by each of these subsystems—information about people, about society, and about performing human services functions in general.

There are four areas of information which are essential to the delivery of human services:

- **Knowledge of history**
- **Knowledge of people**
- **Knowledge of society**
- **Knowledge of resources**

Without a thorough understanding of these four interrelated areas of knowledge, the usefulness of human services is significantly diminished.

Knowledge of History ● Some wise person is reported to have said, "He who ignores history is doomed to repeat it." A sobering thought, to be sure. The importance of a firm understanding of our historical roots is probably self-evident. It's easier to know where we're going when we know where we've been. People learn from their mistakes, and so do professions and societies. The development of the human services profession is a prime example of a society learning from a mistaken pattern and charting a new service course.

Knowledge of People ● An understanding of people—their motivations, dynamics, and strengths—is another area of knowledge that is of crucial importance to the profession. A thorough foundation of knowledge about people—as individuals and as groups—is pivotal to every phase of human services. After all, not only are the individuals to be served people, but the systems to be utilized and/or changed are also made up of people! We should also add that knowing what makes ourselves tick becomes extremely important to the quality of our work in human services. A clear and comfortable self-knowledge is absolutely imperative in working with people and with systems.

Knowledge of Society ● The values, traditions, priorities, problems, trends, and taboos that govern the direction and nature of a society must be fully known and understood if appropriate human services are to be created and sustained by the society itself. We wouldn't get very far in our efforts without a 20/20 perception of the larger society's overriding goals, preferences, and commitments. In addition, knowledge of society and how it works is definitely necessary when change is indicated. Bringing about social change, which human services sometimes does, requires an understanding of the pulse and pressure points within society's legislative machinery. When human services wants to advocate for change, it will need to know where to put its soap-box and where to do its lobbying.

Knowledge of Resources ● All the knowledge of people, history, and society would be of very limited use if human services was ignorant of the resources—fiscal, material, and manpower—that are available to be put into service for people. In our big cities particularly, it is not always easy to keep up with current service innovations and resources. Nor is it easy to learn the way to achieve access to them.

Gaining an adequate knowledge of resources is perhaps the most difficult area for a student of human services to master. Knowledge of history, of people, and of society is more readily to be found in the library and in the classroom. You're left much more on your own initiative to develop and continually update your knowledge of the quality and quantity of service resources. In addition to knowing what services there are and where they are, you must also be well-informed about how good they are, how accessible they are, and how durable they are. This continual researching and reviewing of resources is the basis for forming and maintaining appropriate service linkages to sustain a viable network of human services.

The Human Services Worker

With the new profession has come a new professional: *the human services worker.* While it is true that every person working in any of its subsystems is engaged in human services, there is one trained professional who is neither nurse, social worker, teacher nor psychologist; she is the human services worker. She may, however, work alongside any of her colleagues in any of their systems—and she usually does. For this reason she is considered the "generalist" and each of the others is called a "specialist." This explains why the human services worker has so many other names; i.e., social work assistant; mental health aide; paraprofessional. Her work is often done in conjunction with her colleagues whose training is more specific and advanced in the subsystem. This does not mean, however, that she is "low man on the totem pole." Her skills are unique and different from theirs, intended to augment their work and to integrate the delivery of human services. Her training and formal education are in the broad aspects of human service delivery rather than in the specialized knowledge of any one subsystem. She is, therefore, able to move into and between any of the subsystems to perform her functions as a human services worker. She is, in effect, the human *bridge* between people, systems, and services.

There are four components to the bridge she creates through her work:

Communication • between herself, people, and systems

Understanding • of the person, his problems, and available resources

Relationships • with individuals who need help, as well as with those who can provide help

Strategies • for appropriate and effective action towards problem-solving

The human services worker is a trained professional. However, her personality, maturity, motivation, and life-experiences are considered of at least equal importance to her academic credentials in measuring her usefulness in human services. Her demonstrated competence in bringing services to people is the best indicator of her success in her chosen profession. The quality of her performance and the effect of her efforts on the individual she is trying to serve are what count. Her training involves intensive preparation for human services, requiring mastery of the body of knowledge, theory, and practice skills she will need to help people. Her training is eclectic, generic, and task-oriented to enable her to carry on skillful intervention with an interdisciplinary approach.

It is the human services worker who sees that Mrs. Jones gets the services she needs. For example, if the hospital in which Mrs. Jones' doctor works also employs human services workers (who might be called social worker assistants or something else in that system), this worker would be assigned the task of creating linkages with housing, day care, and welfare systems for Mrs. Jones. We could say that the human services worker, in this way, directs traffic between the subsystems. She is, at the same time, a guide for the individual (like Mrs. Jones) who might otherwise be left to find his or her way through the bureaucratic maze of service systems without a map or compass.

The nature of a person's problems will determine the worker's specific problem-solving tasks. Whatever those tasks turn out to be, the human services worker will pursue them creatively, with a competency based on her experiences, education, skill, and commitment to the principles of her profession.

Human Services Skills

Skill, in the human services profession, means putting into action the field's principles, goals, and knowledge for the purpose of problem-solving. The human services worker is given the responsibility for developing and maintaining a high proficiency in her performance of many professional skills, including:

- techniques for interviewing and counseling
- skill in relating to individuals, groups, and communities
- effectiveness as a change agent
- a capacity for self-scrutiny; adequate self-awareness; and an ability to make professional use of self
- skill in establishing and maintaining stable, useful interdisciplinary relationships
- knowledge of personality, group, and societal dynamics
- an ability to problem-solve and to advocate
- knowledge of teaching, supervisory and research fundamentals
- a capacity for program and system evaluation and planning

The nature of the current needs of the people being served and the available resources for them at any given time will determine the priorities or combinations of skills that the human services worker will be called on to demonstrate.

Her skills must continually be demonstrated in her many professional roles which could include one or more of the following:

Community Planner • working with individuals and groups for the improvement of their community

Consultant • working with other human services subsystems, to assist with their service problems and programs

Broker • helping people reach the services they need and helping systems to be more helpful

Outreach Worker • finding people with problems and referring them to systems for solutions

Advocate • working for the improvement of regulations, policies, and/or laws in order to make systems more accessible to people

Evaluator • assessing individuals' or communities' human services needs and making plans for meeting them

Care Giver • counseling and supporting people with problems in a therapeutic way to promote change either in them or in systems

Mobilizer • working to bring new resources to people

Data Manager • gathering and analyzing information for program planning and evaluation

The human services worker's roles are many. She can be either an administrator, or an assistant to a specialist, or even a clerk. Or she can be assigned one of the tasks described in the list above. Again, the roles she will undertake will be determined by the nature of people's problems, the tasks required to resolve them, and the setting in which the worker is employed at the time. It is possible that, in the course of her career, the human services worker may be asked to undertake all of these roles. Let's just hope it doesn't happen simultaneously!

The Worker's Challenges • Like the profession itself, the human services worker will be demonstrating her competence and skill by meeting four enormous challenges:

- *To Relate* to systems and people
- *To Activate* problem-solving
- *To Integrate* resources and services
- *To Evaluate* human services

The Human Services Career Ladder

This section will necessarily be brief because, to a large extent, the building of the human services career ladder isn't finished yet! The new profession has, in an incredibly short period of time, defined itself and created a new professional. There are many, many jobs open and waiting for beginning human services workers now. There is room for advancement and additional education for every worker throughout the field.

It isn't easy to outline the steps up the human services career ladder. The path is much clearer in the rest of the academic world, for example, where one moves from the associate degree to the bachelor's degree to master's degree to doctorate. This step-by-step credentialing is usually followed faithfully by all the others engaged in human services subsystems. Undoubtedly, graduate education will come to the human services worker, too—in time. Whether we share our society's "credential mania" or disparage it, I'm afraid we're not likely to escape it. In less than a decade, over 200 colleges across the United States have opened programs leading to an associate degree in human services. Can advanced programs for refining and expanding our skills be far behind?

To a very large extent, every human services worker who is just now beginning her career will be shaping and directing the future course of her profession, its educational requirements, its impact on society, and its effectiveness as a bridge between people and services. It is a formidable challenge and an exciting time for all of us.

Just remember: *people before paper!*

chapter two

A History of Human Services

Throughout history, every civilization has asked the question, *What is helpful?* and has provided human services in accordance with society's answer. The answer itself has been based on the prevailing attitudes about helpfulness at the time. People have always needed human services, of course. But, history reveals that the supply of human services has never even nearly equalled the demand for them.

In this world, there have always been two basic groups of people: *the Haves and the Have-nots.* Until recently in human history, there were only two classes of people: the rich and the poor. In fact, in most of the contemporary world, there are still only two classes. In the western world, the rise of the middle class has significantly influenced the mushrooming of human services. But, human services began to evolve much earlier. Over time, more and more human services have been made accessible to people. It is important to understand how this occurred.

Clearly, the rich have always had access to all the human services they might want or need. They simply had better buying power. In earlier eras, even services like medical care, adequate housing, free education, or income maintenance were not readily accessible to the poor. Services were not accessible to them because they had no money. This imbalance in the distribution of human services spotlights a fundamental fact of human history: *inequality.* Because inequality has been so deeply rooted in every society, there have always been the Haves and the Have-nots, and there has also been an unequal distribution of wealth, resources, knowledge, and power among people.

Ironically, it has been traditional that the people least in need of human services have always had the most access to them. This seems to be a common chord in the history of each human services subsystem, from medicine to recreation. Therefore, instead of tracing the historical development of each individual human services subsystem, we will look more closely at the growth of the profession as a whole, and at the increasing accessibility of human services over time to more and more people.

BUILDING THE HUMAN SERVICES BRIDGE

The central question in the history of human services seems to be whether human services are a *right of* or a *gift* to the individual. The root of this "right" versus "gift" question is, of course, the inequality that has been inherent in every major civilization to the present. No large society has yet dedicated itself to insuring total social and economic equality—or equal access to human services—for all its members. Instead, societal efforts have been launched to at least make inequality more bearable for those with the least of society's benefits. Consequently, no society has yet achieved the basic goals and principles of the human services profession. Nevertheless, every society has shown at least some concern about "What is helpful?" and some interest in providing human services more equitably.

There is room for a good deal of conjecture about why societies have been motivated to provide human services at all. It would have been very easy for the Haves to provide only for themselves and to have ignored the needs of the Have-nots altogether. Was each successive society motivated to provide human services out of a basic humanitarian compassion and sense of justice? Or, did the Haves in the society view and support human services for the Have-nots as a means of social control?

Compassion and Control

It has often occurred to me that if people were asked to choose between compassion and Cadillacs, there wouldn't be any leftover Cadillacs. It is probably most accurate to conclude that society, over the centuries, has developed and supported the expansion of human services for several reasons:

- **to preserve the social order**

  and

- **to respond to human need**

Society could not long endure if large numbers of its members were dissatisfied to the point of revolution. Also, society generally fosters some sense of responsibility among its members for one another and stimulates some feeling of commonality between them (to a greater or lesser extent). It is this unlikely combination of motivating forces—compassion and control—(with all their inherent conflicts) that has fostered the steady growth and development of human services.

Two-Track Helping

Throughout history, whether it has been known as charity, justice, duty, social welfare, or human services, the task has been the same: to promote the enhancement of daily life for individuals and for families. Obviously, the Have-nots needed a lot more services and resources to enhance their lives. And, society did increasingly provide added resources (whatever its motivation). However, because of the split in society between the Haves and the Have-nots, human services developed as a two-track system: one network of services for each group. While the human services available to the Haves could be refined and improved because of the plentiful financial and other resources available to them, the growth of human services for the Have-nots was closely related to solving another issue: overcoming the deprivations and the social problems rooted in economic, racial, and social inequality which confronted the Have-nots. Therefore, the growth of human services was closely related to the existence of both poverty and inequality in society. It was also very significantly influenced by the attitudes of the Haves toward the Have-nots.

A review of the changes in attitudes towards human services over time, and the resulting developments in the field will point up quite clearly that, as the relative positions of the Haves and the

Have-nots changed, there has been a steadily increasing investment by society in providing human services. Furthermore, as society has begun to attack the roots of its inequality, there has been a stronger commitment to provide human services as a "right" for every member of society.

EARLY HISTORY

Every early society, usually through its religious practices, concerned itself with regulating behavior and attitudes towards people in need of human services, particularly social welfare. The major tenets of every religion have included some prescription similar to the Golden Rule, "Do unto others as you would have them do unto you." The laws of Moses; the teachings of Buddha; the code of Hammurabi; as well as Hindu, Egyptian, Greek, and Roman social philosophies provide additional examples of those societies' interest in guiding helpful behavior.

Throughout history it was emphasized that it was the duty of the Haves to help the Have-nots. Conversely, it was the right of the Have-nots to expect assistance from their fellows, according to social custom. The rights and duties of both groups then were clear-cut. There was, of course, a very definite limit set on how much help should be expected. For centuries, the limit was set at the lowest possible level for survival—*subsistence*.

It was usually the responsibility of religious organizations and their representatives to mediate the distribution of social welfare between the Haves and the Have-nots and to redistribute what was given by those who had enough to those who had extremely little of the essentials of life. There seems to have been little concern with determining why those with almost nothing were in that predicament. Nor was there (at least long ago) a negative attitude toward the deprived person, or blame put on him for his own deprivation. That would come later.

Modern human services ideology today probably has its closest roots in the Judeo-Christian ethic which strongly affirmed the rights of the deprived to help and the duty of the comfortable to provide them with help. It is interesting to note that in the early Christian church, when people had neither property nor poverty, everybody provided equally for one another. However, as society and the church grew more complex and prospered, this simple equality seems to have been lost. A two-class society emerged in Europe: the rich and the poor (the Haves and the Have-nots, of course). Throughout the Middle Ages, it was the church that provided much of the human services to the Have-nots. However, its attitude toward the people it felt responsibility for serving underwent a subtle change. The church preached the doing of one's "Christian duty" as a means of salvation in those days. Implicit in that message was the notion that helping the Have-nots was like some sort of insurance policy for the next life. Clearly, giving this sort of "ulterior motive" to helpfulness was a first step in the dehumanizing of the Have-nots that followed.

From their pulpits, religious leaders during the Middle Ages continued to teach their parishioners that doing good works was a means to an end. The sermons never mentioned that the Have-nots had any *right* to expect help. The Haves promptly got the message and forgot that the Have-nots were just as human as they were! Certainly some compassion remained. In fact, as the church became more highly organized it founded many new human service delivery systems including institutions for the poor; orphanages; homes for the aged; and residences for the handicapped. These institutional services were first located within monasteries and later at independent sites around the community. Forerunners of modern hospitals were called "hotêls-Dieu" and were administered by religious orders in France.

Two saints—St. Thomas Aquinas and St. Francis d'Assisi—might well be called the first human services professionals because of their efforts to bring services to people during that time. However, belief in the dignity and worth of the Have-nots was no longer shared by the less saintly masses. People were helping as much from their own self-interest as anything, it began to seem. If providing human services was often done with a grudge (and probably for the wrong reasons), it was, nevertheless, being done diligently.

The battle for dominance in society was waged between church and state throughout the Middle Ages. Both warring factions were determined to govern society without the interference of the other. One area in which the state sought to wrench control from the church was in the provision of human services to the Have-nots. The state knew that the church was strong enough to demand that its parishioners *tithe* (donate 10% of their incomes for the work of the church).

The state wanted very much to undercut that power. Until the end of the Middle Ages, the church retained its control of human service activities, for the most part, and each parish or locality was given responsibility for meeting, at least minimally, the needs of its parishioners. The state, however, steadily increased its efforts to direct those activities itself. For example, as early as 800 A.D., Charlemagne made it illegal to give alms to those who could work. His ruling was, he said, intended to preserve the social order (and to protect the Haves, which he didn't say). Those were feudal times and that social system depended on serfs staying on the manor as a source of free labor. By making begging difficult, it was assumed that fewer serfs would leave the manors for freedom, much to the consternation of the lords of the manor.

By the end of the Middle Ages, the Haves no longer looked upon the Have-nots with understanding or much compassion. They were viewed more as a "necessary evil." By the fourteenth century, classification of the Have-nots had begun. In society's mind there were two kinds of Have-nots:

The Able-bodied Poor • individuals who were considered physically fit for work

The Impotent Poor • children, widows, the aged, and the handicapped

A clear distinction was made between the two groups. The latter was called the "worthy poor" and the able-bodied were scorned. It apparently never occurred to many people that the choice between serfdom (which was virtual slavery) and begging wasn't much choice at all. Nor was it likely that jobs were plentiful for those brave souls who did leave their manors in search of another, better way of life. To be sure, there were some beggars who chose begging as a relatively easy line of work, but it is simply implausible that this was the case for most.

It is interesting to observe that as society approached more modern times it seems to have been side-tracked into wondering more about *why* it should be helpful than *how* it might help. This trend would, unfortunately, continue for some time. As a matter of fact, there are those of us who believe that human services efforts today are still side-tracked for the very same reason.

Europe: 1500–1900

As Europe came out of the Dark Ages, it was confronted by society in turbulent transition, not unlike our own modern changing times. Beginning in the sixteenth century, the very core of society was being transformed entirely. The most significant factors in bringing about this metamorphosis were:

- the end of the feudal system

- the decline of church power

- the dawn of industrialization

It was a time of social, religious, and economic upheaval. The Protestant Reformation in the sixteenth century heightened the conflict between church and state and was a decisive factor in the state finally overshadowing the authority of the church by the close of that century. Hand-in-hand with the Reformation came the Industrial Revolution. Together, these forces would totally alter European society within a few hundred years. The impact of those changes on human services was not inconsequential.

In England, when Henry VIII confiscated the church's vast properties, he also took many of the monasteries that had provided human services to the Have-nots. In addition, he eliminated the parochial system of distributing alms within parishes. It therefore became necessary for the English government to take over these human services facilities and functions and to develop a system of public welfare services, including income maintenance. The Statute of 1536 established responsibility for development of such a system within the government. Shortly afterwards, the Statute of 1572 reinforced the government's responsibility to people who could not be self-sufficient. Related legislation continued to be enacted until it was all incorporated in a code during the reign of Queen Elizabeth I.

The Elizabethan Poor Law of 1601 was to become the framework for human services both in England and the United States until the

1800s. The Poor Law identified three groups of Have-nots:

- *The Able-bodied*—who were forced to work
- *The Impotent Poor*—who were aged or infirm, and mothers for whom relief was provided
- *Dependent Children*—who, because they were orphaned or abandoned, became state wards

The Poor Law specified that the human services needs of an individual in any of these three groups was first the responsibility of his family. If the family was unable to provide for him, it became the state's responsibility to do so. There were two main systems established for providing human services: indoor relief and outdoor relief. *Indoor relief* required that the deprived person who needed shelter and other essentials live in an almshouse (or poorhouse). If it was decided that the person was able-bodied, he was sent to a workhouse where his labor was forced. *Outdoor relief* was the alternative to the poorhouse. Under its provisions, a family needing help could be maintained at home and the community would make "in-kind" contributions of food and clothing to the household. Medical care was less frequently given. Other services, like education, were unheard of then. Money was almost never provided directly.

Early Bureaucracy

Having determined that when there was no viable family, the deprived individual became the state's and the community's responsibility, it followed that a system was needed to administer relief-giving under government supervision. To accomplish this, a network of "overseers of the poor" was created. This network was, no doubt, the forerunner of the modern welfare bureaucracy. The deprived person seeking help had to register in his community. His application needed the approval of an overseer before relief was granted. In addition to determining eligibility, the overseer was also expected to collect the "poor tax" which existed in each community to support relief measures, with private philanthropic contributions as supplements. (The contemporary welfare worker doesn't have to double as tax-collector nowadays, but her tasks have not changed much in three hundred years, it seems.)

By the end of the seventeenth century in Europe, society had changed its thinking about "What is helpful?" several times. The *mutual-aid* concept of Biblical times gave way to an attitude of reluctant acceptance of responsibility by the Haves for the Have-nots. In the process, the two groups moved further and further apart and a bureaucracy was put in place between them.

Impact of Technology

The advent of industrialism on the ashes of the feudal system not only brought another change in society's view of human services, but also redefined man's perspective on himself and the world around him. To say the least, life became a lot less predictable! Previously, there had been lords and serfs and a rather simple order to things. People knew where they stood with each other and what to expect from the world during their lifetimes. Then, rather abruptly, the world, soon after discovering itself to be round, promptly turned upside-down! The advent of industry demanded a new social order. Machines rapidly replaced craftsmen and required migration of masses of people to urban centers where factories sprang up and required manpower to run them.

Industrialization brought another shift in perspective: people began to suspect that, through their earthly labors they might expect their rewards in the here-and-now, instead of waiting patiently for eternity, as the church had counseled them to do. Industrialization brought a new, striving middle class to society and introduced a new emphasis on another concept in human relationships: competition. By the close of the seventeenth century, the accumulation of wealth had become a virtue, and poverty had become a vice. A man's worth in society was measured by his effectiveness in manipulating the market place. The *profit motive* burst on the scene with immediate support from the Haves, of course. It is clear that if a society measures its members' worth in terms of their wealth, those who are not wealthy are going to be given very little respect. This is certainly what happened as industrialization advanced with the times.

Society was structured then, as it is now, in such a way that not all had equal access to the accumulation of wealth. Only those who did have such access were successful and powerful. They were able to utilize the labors of the others without sharing fairly the jointly-earned wealth with any of them. As people lost faith in the innate dignity of their fellow men and left behind them a sense of duty towards others, they felt little reluctance in using the labors of the Have-nots for as long and as cheaply as possible to further the interests of the Haves. The lucky ones during industrialization seemed to look on the Have-nots with an attitude of "I'm OK, but I'm not at all sure about you anymore."

With such an attitude, it would seem almost predictable that human services should have been abolished altogether for those who couldn't pay top dollar. There were two factors, however, that encouraged the continued growth, rather than the dissolution of human services:

- **The rise of the middle class**

    and

- **The rapid urbanization of society**

Together, these new societal forces prompted a significant increase in human services. Without them, the prevailing attitude of the Haves might indeed have resulted in more, not less, inequality and less, not more, human services.

There are those who argue that even today the middle class could be considered Have-nots because of the persisting imbalance in the distribution of income in society and the disproportionate amount of control that the very rich have over society's resources. While that may be true, it is also a fact that the demands of the middle class for increased access to human services of all kinds did stimulate the rapid growth of the profession over the last two hundred years. As people were able to earn more money, they also gained enough power to demand—and receive—more human services. This happened throughout the human services subsystems. People, particularly those living in urban areas where they were less self-sufficient than they had been on the farm, needed and wanted better housing, better medical care, better education, and a host of other human services.

Power and Services

Unquestionably, access to human services is essentially a matter of *power*. People with power get what they ask for. People without power have to go without much of anything. There are, of course, all kinds of power—besides actual dollars. The Have-nots have had the power to generate some human services throughout history because society wants, above all, to maintain order. The Poor Law of 1601 had been created not so much as a benevolent gesture but more as a means of social control after a period of famine, inflation, and economic insufficiency had threatened to tear apart the existing social order. (Our own American Social Security Act in 1935 had similar origins.) In retrospect, it is clear that three interacting factors have stimulated the development and expansion of human services across all classes in society:

- **the society's attitudes towards helpfulness**
- **the relative distribution of wealth and power**
- **people's changing needs as society evolves**

The development of human services is, in a way, a reflection of the power struggle between the Haves and the Have-nots. When the society devalued the Have-nots and felt little moral obligation toward them there was little hope for the sponsorship of adequate and equitable human services. It was obviously in the self-interest of the Haves to maintain a class of Have-nots as the labor supply. Even though most of the Have-nots were working people, their employment didn't make their misery less acute or their access to human services any closer. In early industrialization, there were no labor unions, or minimum wages, no prohibitions against child labor, or forty-hour weeks. Employment was no insurance against deprivation.

Also, the normal business cycles in their lulls drove much of the labor force to apply for government assistance or philanthropy. The appalling increase in industry-related accidents, disease, and death did the same. Because of these side-effects of industrialization, English taxes for "poor relief" tripled between 1776 and 1832. The Haves begrudged these taxes with increasing vehemence and apparently found it more convenient to view the Have-nots as "unworthy" than to abandon their fierce competitiveness and their attitude towards the Have-nots as non-human labor commodities. It was about this time that the victims of inequality in the social order were beginning to be blamed for their own deprivation.

Economic Boom and Backlash

While the economic developments during Industrialization were obviously of major consequence in reshaping European society, there were simultaneous far-reaching developments in religion that reinforced people's new attitudes towards themselves, each other, help-fulness, and their world, in general. The Protestant Reformation swept across Europe with gusto and introduced not only a new religious faith, but a new social ideology, as well. Known as the *Protestant Ethic* (sometimes called the Work Ethic or the Puritan Ethic), it preached a set of values, elaborated as time went on, which served to reinforce the commandments of industrialization. Namely, it advocated that wealth was virtuous; poverty contemptable. In this framework, hard work was seen as the road to salvation. It also stressed that wealth was God's reward for goodness. Conversely, poverty was seen as divine punishment for some sort of "moral flaw." While charity was not disapproved since it was still viewed as further evidence of an individual's goodness, the Protestant Ethic as taught by John Calvin maintained that it was God's will for the Have-nots to be in those straits. How very convenient. Thoughts about any existing inequality in income or human services distribution could be handily dismissed as "God's will." And, after all, who would tamper with "God's will"?

Indeed, as modern times approached, the Haves became convinced that they deserved all they got and that the Have-nots de-

John Calvin.

served next to nothing because God (and the market place) ordained it. By 1834, in England the ever-increasing needs of the Have-nots were becoming more irksome to the Calvinist Haves and they finally rebelled. To cite Disraeli, a politician of the time, with the passage of the Poor Law Reform measures that year, it actually became a crime to be poor! The intent of the new law was to discourage the expansion of help to the Have-nots by making eligibility for help much more difficult and by making the help itself as meager as possible. The concept of *less eligibility* was introduced. This was a principle stating that the amount of assistance provided to any Have-nots must be lower than the lowest wage received by any working person. In other words, the Have-nots were not to be allowed even the lowest standard of living enjoyed by a member of the work force. A person's productivity was, indeed, a measure of his worth in other people's eyes. It apparently didn't matter much that the individual who was not or could not be productive for whatever reason still shared the same needs for human services as his employable neighbor.

The year 1834 may seem very long ago, but the doctrine of "Less Eligibility" is still very much alive. As recently as October 1974, the *New York Times* summarized a study of New York City's welfare recipients revealing that this group of Have-nots is still subjected to the dictates of "Less Eligibility." For example, the article noted that in 1971 the amount of relief available for a family in need equalled no more than two-thirds of the income determined as an adequate standard of living in the United States. Is it still a crime to be poor? Is it still the individual's own fault? Should human services, therefore, be withheld from all but the "worthy" working Haves? The answers to those questions are still ambiguous and the uneven development of human services up to contemporary times is a result of that ambiguity.

America's Human Services

The New World, as the Pilgrims and early settlers found it, was hardly the "land of opportunity" as we often tend to glorify it. The climate was harsh and the conditions were severe. Each young colony faced great odds against survival and each had a number of social problems for which an adequate supply of human services simply didn't exist. So much for our contented, turkey-stuffed Thanksgiving Day illusions!

Interior of a New England's pioneer home.

36

The majority of the earliest Americans were poor and, therefore, Have-nots. Some had even been expelled from Europe because they were dependent on "poor relief" there. The hardships of America as well as its early wars—French-and-Indian; Revolutionary—added to the colonists' deprivations and created a growing demand for increased human services.

The early Americans believed that there would always necessarily be deprivation (because some people had a "moral flaw") and that the Have-nots' very existence provided an opportunity to do good works. The Protestant Ethic was dutifully followed on this side of the Atlantic as European religious and economic forces converged again in the New World. The Elizabethan Poor Laws were adopted in the earliest days of this nation—as early as 1642 in Plymouth. In this way, the United States established almost immediately a public relief system supplemented by voluntary (private) philanthropy. People who were unable to provide for their own needs were called "indigents" and up through the 1800s were helped in one of four ways generally:

- *Outdoor Relief*—where "in-kind" contributions were provided in their own homes
- *Indoor Relief*—where Almshouses were established
- A *contract system*—in which the local government and a local family would board an indigent at community expense
- *Auctions-in-reverse*—in which the person was sent to the lowest bidder who gave basic human services in exchange for the indigent's free labor

Although outdoor relief was most common, the other forms of helping had their place, too. Obviously, the attitude towards the Have-not was a pivotal factor in determining how to help him.

There was, as there had been in Europe, a certain harshness associated with helpfulness particularly after the official birth of the nation in 1776. Before then (as had also been true in Europe), when the society was young and simple, its humanitarian instincts and its helpfulness seem to have been more in evidence. This case of history repeating itself leads one to speculate even further about the importance of power in the development of societies and human interrelationships as well as the growth of the human services profession which ultimately resulted.

Laissez Faire

In 1776, while the English were bemoaning the loss of the American colonies, they were also intrigued by the writings of a man named Adam Smith. This Englishman authored *Wealth of Nations* and fathered the economic concept of *laissez faire* which is sometimes called "free market economy." Its core theory is that the economy would be self-regulating and fruitful if allowed to function without any governmental interference or controls. Its implication is that business interests could guide society perfectly well to everyone's benefit *if* government is not allowed to restrict the activities of the market place. A corresponding social philosophy grew out of this theory which is neatly summed up in the adage, "Live and let live." Laissez faire economists strongly criticized the concept of human services as a "right" and were particularly against the provision of any relief measures, arguing that they were counterproductive to economic development.

In 1798, Thomas Malthus, another Englishman, wrote his now famous "Essay on the Principle of Population," in which he warned that while the population was growing geometrically, the world's food supply was only growing arithmetically. In other words, the demand for food would increase far more rapidly than the supply. Malthus concluded that society was in danger of overpopulation. He felt that society was compounding the problem by giving human services to the Have-nots. It is easy to refute Malthus today by citing developments in both the field of food-production and the science of family-planning. At that time, however, people became very concerned by his pessimistic prophecies.

The American Dream

Taken together, the theories of Smith and Malthus were certainly pivotal in shifting attitudes in society even further than ever from egalitarian helpfulness and the belief that human services might be everybody's entitlement. In England, the 1834 Poor Law Reform bears witness to this. In America, Smith and Malthus also enjoyed great popularity while their theories negatively influenced contemporary thinking about the equitable distribution of human services.

Simultaneously, something else was happening in the United States, too: The West was being won. Americans adopted a "frontier spirit" and a staunch faith in "rugged individualism" for the occasion. These attitudes, along with an affection for "American ingenuity" were incorporated into the American version of the Protestant Ethic which we often call the *American Dream*. This is society's "dominant ethos," and although it has undergone some modification since the frontier days, its major components remain largely unchanged and still seem to be almost universally accepted among today's Americans. The American Dream holds that

- **The validity of the Protestant Ethic is self-evident; success comes with hard work; i.e., "Anyone can be President" . . . if he works hard enough.**

- **Rugged individualism is another key to success and salvation. People should depend only on themselves. Self-help is the gospel.**

- **The frontier spirit encourages exploration, achievement, and empire-building.**

Now there is nothing inherently wrong with the American Dream. Its positive effect on creativity and productivity can be convincingly argued. For many it has been the model for success. But, what about the others? Has there really been enough "room at the top" for every hard-working American? I suspect that the successful ones have troubled themselves little with questions like these. After all, according to their social philosophy, success was virtuous; dependency a vice. Secretly, I'm quite sure that those at the top were quite pleased that there wasn't access to great fortunes for the vast majority of people in this country. Privately, the Haves probably viewed the Have-nots with contempt and paternalism. Publicly, however, sponsoring human services and giving charitable contributions was to become a badge of social recognition. It became a status symbol to be a generous philanthropist. It wasn't that anyone particularly thought that a Have-not had any right to be helped. It was for the benefit of the giver that help was really provided. And, as in earlier eras in

Europe, helpfulness was targeted at lessening the effects of the fundamental inequality of the society rather than at rooting out the inequality itself.

Social Darwinism

After the Civil War, attitudes towards human services in the United States shifted once again. Massive immigration, rapid industrialization, growing urbanization, and the tensions of the times yielded growing evidence that the Have-nots might be more the victims of an unstable economy than of their own "moral flaws." Such suspicions were to be put to rest for a time, however, by the emergence of yet another social theory, *Social Darwinism*.

This philosophy was an outgrowth (a corruption?) of Charles Darwin's biological concept of evolution and the process of "natural selection". Herbert Spencer, also an Englishman, tailored Darwin's biological theories to explain social and economic phenomena. It was Herbert Spencer who actually coined the phrase, "survival of the fittest" by which he meant that it was no less than a law of nature that the most fit people in society would survive and that the least fit would not. This, he proclaimed, was the natural order of things. He recommended that if the so-called natural order was left to operate unimpeded that eventually it would create a society of more perfect people. (Sounds like a later conception of a "master race," doesn't it?) By the 1870s, American intellectuals were fascinated by the notion of man's perfectibility as implied in the theory of evolution.

Spencer's Social Darwinism represented a marriage of convenience between the Protestant Ethic and laissez-faire economics which, he was certain, was blessed by natural law. According to Spencer, skill, intellect, and self-control increased the individual's power to adapt successfully to society and made a person "fit." He assumed that anyone unable to meet all his own needs independently was simply "unfit." On this assumption, he urged the abandonment of the poor laws and other state-supported human services, warning that if the "unfit" were helped too much, society would face a calamity of the "survival of the *un*fittest." Social Darwinism became almost immediately accepted during the post-Civil War "Gilded Age" in America. It suited the rather hedonistic times so well. Nature favored the fit, Spencer had told them. So, if they were fit, they should simply enjoy and not worry about the unfit.

Spencer had also reintroduced Darwin's observation that a "struggle for existence" goes on in life. Spencer acknowledged the struggle and maintained that the struggle could only be won by the most fit, the most adaptable. The conclusion drawn by the Social Darwinists was that competition was the natural law of life. Consequently, further justification of inequality became unnecessary to them.

The flaws in Social Darwinism are readily apparent when one starts to question exactly what is meant by the term "fit." To Spencer, fitness seems to have been synonymous with usefulness to the market place. But, isn't there more to dignity and human worth than that? It's true that there is, in nature, a struggle for existence to which we are all subject. But, isn't *cooperation* an even more dominating law of nature than *competition* is? Well, as they say, "People believe what they want to believe" or, perhaps, what they *need* to believe. Most nineteenth century Americans were easily convinced that supporting expanded human services was no concern of theirs. If they were fit, they took care of their own needs and didn't worry about anyone else.

From the history of social welfare, a good example of Social Darwinism's influence can be drawn. In the beginning of the 19th century, the New York Society for the Prevention of Pauperism identified the following causes of deprivation: excessive drinking, ignorance, lack of thrift, "imprudent and hasty marriages," lotteries, pawnbrokers, "houses of ill fame," and even "the numerous charitable institutions." As the century went on, society became more convinced that providing human services seemed to undermine the motivation of the Have-nots to become more productive. The real roots of the problems confronting the so-called "unfit"—industrial accidents; ill health; low wages; loss of breadwinner—were almost entirely ignored for many decades.

Not only were the Have-nots considered weak and "unfit," they were, paradoxically, also feared. Identified as the "dangerous classes," they were given governmental relief (at bare subsistence levels) more out of society's fear of revolt than anything else—as usual. The Haves had reason for renewed fear. Their prosperity, unparalleled in history which they, the minority, were enjoying during the Gilded Age, was being attained at the expense and the back-breaking labor of the majority. By the end of the nineteenth century, at least one out of every eight Americans was living in dire poverty without access to most of the fundamental human services! That this could be true in the "land of plenty" defies logical explanation except for the fact that there was no effective government regulation of resources, income distribution, or human services to insure that *every* citizen could enjoy the fruits of modern, industrialized America.

Tycoon Times

Laissez faire and Social Darwinism dominated American social attitudes right into the twentieth century. Neither of these theories had much respect for equality or humanitarian concerns. The tycoons of the day—Andrew Carnegie, John Rockefeller, and others—were looked upon as living proof of the "every man for himself" creed. Such "self-made men" were the heroes of the times. Their rags-to-riches stories were presented as ample evidence of what an industrious, inventive person could accomplish if he tried hard and wasn't impeded by government. Self-sufficiency was applauded over everything else.

Realistically, of course, self-sufficiency was not entirely possible in an urbanized society. People, when they moved from their farms into town, also moved from independence to interdependence. The notion of near-total self-sufficiency was reserved for Mr. Carnegie and Mr. Rockefeller. Others—in the middle class and in the lower class—were increasingly dependent on society to meet their needs for human services.

Ironically and fortunately, society does not always practice what it preaches. Even though Social Darwinism enjoyed great popularity here, very few proponents seriously considered doing away with all human services. On the contrary, human services had another growth spurt. Indeed, by the close of the nineteenth century, there had been substantial movement in every branch of the human services. Not only were services improved, but they were made accessible to more and more people.

As the twentieth century approached, society was beginning to understand its people's interdependence and was supporting the expansion of human services needed to meet their new needs for satisfying life in the cities to which they were moving. Society was also beginning to recognize that the need for human services was very often multiplied by people's new, urban environments. Consequently, society moved closer towards accepting that some human services were, indeed, the right of every American. As society ac-

New York City, 1889.

cepted the responsibility for fulfilling more and more human service needs, there were expansions in each of the subsystems as a result. Old ideas die hard, however. As the twentieth century approached, attitudes about human services were not entirely in favor of a proliferation of them. Nevertheless, things were slowly, but surely moving in that direction.

The only thing really constant in a society is *change*. No one walks in the same societal stream twice. By the close of the nineteenth century, societal forces were converging once again to promote changes which would impact on social attitudes and, therefore, on human services. In the economic sphere, there was growing awareness of the monolithic power which business interest had acquired. There was growing criticism of this. To discourage monopolies' control of the economy in the future, the Sherman Antitrust Act became law in 1890. Pure laissez-faire economics was very definitely on the decline. It had benefited too few at the expense of too many.

At the same time, biologists and other scientists were opening the heredity-versus-environment controversy and beginning to give appropriate credence to the effect of environment on living things, including people. This new attitude among intellectuals was by no means an overnight success in altering the thinking of the average person, but the proverbial handwriting was on the wall, just the same. The Protestant Ethic and the American Dream were very much alive and well. But, events were to come which would bring some fundamental change to those philosophies and to attitudes about human services.

Scanning History • Looking back from antiquity to modern times, it is clear that the need for human services has been a fact of life from day one. So, apparently, has unequal access to those services. Every generation has been confronted with human need and with the realities of inequality and gaps in human services. Each has drawn its own conclusions about helpfulness and each has adopted an attitude about human services which was most in harmony with the society's dominant interests and values at that particular point in history. This will probably always be true. Whether society decides that human services are a "gift" from the Haves to the Have-nots or are the fundamental "right" of every member of the society will continue to be determined more by the priorities of its majority of people than by any appeal to human rights.

Whether a society will take responsibility for eradicating inequality and enhancing every individual's life will also be decided by the priorities for human services adopted by the majority. It was ever thus, and clearly it continues to be so in the twentieth century. As we have now seen, the answer to "What is helpful?" is neither definite nor is it necessarily permanent. On the contrary, the answer changes as the society changes. It probably always will. And, consequently, so will the accessibility and adequacy of human services.

BIBLIOGRAPHY

Bremner, Robert. *From the Depths.* New York: New York University Press, 1967.

Curti, Merle. *The Growth Of American Thought.* New York: Harper and Row, 1964.

De Schweinitz, Karl. *England's Road to Social Security.* Philadelphia: University of Pennsylvania Press, 1943.

Friedlander, Walter A. and Apte, Robert A. *Introduction to Social Welfare.* 4th ed. Englewood Cliffs, N.J.: Prentice-Hall, Inc., 1974.

Hofstadter, Richard. *Social Darwinism in American Thought.* Boston: Beacon Press, 1944.

Polanyi, Karl. *The Great Transformation.* Boston: Beacon Press, 1957.

Riis, Jacob. *How the Other Half Lives.* New York: Scribner's Sons, 1890.

Schlesinger, Arthur and White, Morton, eds. *Paths of American Thought.* Boston: Houghton Mifflin, 1963.

Trattner, Walter. *From Poor Law to Welfare State.* New York: Free Press, 1974.

chapter three

Human Services Today

America welcomed the twentieth century with great expectations. And, well it should have. In a relatively short span of history, America had already accomplished a great deal. By 1900, most of its people were enjoying a standard of living and a social mobility that their contemporaries in other parts of the world couldn't hope to expect at that time. By the early 1900s, there were 100 million Americans of whom 50% were living in urban areas. America was emerging as a world power and a center for inventive technology which was gaining world-wide respect. The increasing prestige and affluence of the United States pleased its own citizens most of all, naturally enough. In the space of a few years, Americans would invent an array of technological innovations and proceed to revolutionize technology and their own futures.

TURN OF THE CENTURY

While it is clear that America came to this century bearing wondrous gifts and holding great promise, there was also a persisting inadequacy in the society. Although human services had been expanding as the nineteenth century drew to a close, there was still a very short supply of human services for most people. The notion, often put forth in those days, that there was no longer any scarcity in America was simply unfounded. There was a scarcity of human services very definitely. In fact, as the 1900s arrived, at least 12% of Americans were severely deprived of even the most essential services for survival. These ten million people were living in abject poverty, without decent housing or medical care. Among them, illiteracy was almost universal as was malnutrition. Perhaps no one noticed.

A number of professionals in many allied human services disciplines did notice. In particular, the *Settlement House Movement* in social welfare (as well as comparable efforts in other fields) helped to bring human services to that 12% of Americans in dire need while also spotlighting the more general human services needs of the entire population in the United States. The philosophy of the Settlement House Movement, begun in the 1880s, is a good example of early human services thinking. Settlement house workers were certain that when an individual was in need it was the responsibility of society and its social systems to provide for him. Furthermore, those workers were convinced that most of the individual's problems in providing for his own needs were created by his environment, not by his own inadequacy. At the time, most helping efforts focused on "helping people to help themselves." The settlement house professionals recognized, however, that it would be necessary to focus first on improving the social environment. That, they felt, was a prerequisite to enhancing the quality of life for people through the provision of human services.

A typical settlement house, such as the famous Hull House opened by Jane Addams in Chicago, became a hub of community activity. In the settlement house, professionals saw the struggles people had to merely survive. Adequate food, clothing, health care, education and recreation were not accessible. Settlement house workers responded to the need they saw by stimulating the development of a range of needed human services. By the early 1900s, the *Settlement House Movement*—and the hard facts it brought to light about human needs—began to have some significant positive impact on society's attitudes toward "What is helpful?" and toward the expansion of human services.

With the settlement house professionals leading the way, society was beginning to point a finger at its own economy as the cause of inadequacy and inequity in human services. The issues came to the forefront at a Conference of Charities and Correction in 1912. At the Conference, a number of proposals were presented for improving the quality of life for Americans. Recommended were:

- **a minimum wage**
- **an eight-hour day (at least for women and children!)**
- **a six-day work week**
- **limitations on night work**

- pensions for 65-year-olds
- industrial safety standards
- workmen's compensation
- unemployment insurance
- prohibition of child labor

Also recommended was an acknowledgement by government that it was every American family's *right* to live in a safe, sanitary home at a moderate rent. Eventually, of course, these recommendations were made law. But, not without strong opposition from business interests who saw that such provisions for laborers would cut sharply into their profit margins. Businessmen were rather unaccustomed to viewing their labor supply as human beings with their own rights to human services and to a decent standard of living.

EMERGING HUMAN SERVICES THINKING

Modern-day human services and society as a whole owe a great debt to the many early pioneering efforts of professionals like the settlement house workers and others in the fields of mental health and public health, particularly. Those early human services professionals led the way toward meaningful social change by identifying a model for service upon which to build. They gave us two clear-cut goals:

- **Prevent deprivation**
- **Promote the enhancement of human life**

These twin goals are, of course, the cornerstone of human services. The earlier professionals' commitment to them gave us a clear path to follow. In Jane Addams' day that incomparable lady developed an incredibly impressive range of human services in her Chicago neighborhood: kindergartens, an employment bureau, art classes, basic education, vocational training programs, health services, day care, and even a bank! Such early efforts at comprehensiveness in human services have also provided those of us in the field today with an understanding of how almost boundless the scope of human services really is, when we attempt the practical application of those fundamental goals.

The philosophy of human services, as we know it today, is based on a deep conviction that justice and equality are *all* people's rights. Then and now, human services places "people motives" over the profit motive and seeks to demonstrate as much flexibility and creativity as necessary to insure people's rights to adequate and accessible human services. Human services, since the turn of the century, has concerned itself as much with the impact of the environment on the individual as on the individual's immediate needs. As a result of those pioneering efforts in human services, we know that it is not possible to insure the achievement of the basic human services goals without paying close attention to the forces in society which mold and shape people's lives, particularly the forces of economy and ecology.

Interdisciplinary Beginnings

The first two decades of the twentieth century were noted as the time of materialism and the Jazz Age. They were also the era of the Progressive Movement in the area of human services. During those twenty years, it became clear that meaningful reform had to come in society, not through charitable acts, but through sound legislation. Sometimes called the *Social Justice Movement,* its advocates campaigned actively for the labor controls already discussed, as well as for a very broad range of improvements in every human services area including: public health, education, social services, housing, and mental health. During this heyday of the Progressives and the Muckrakers, great gains were made to improve the quality of life for all Americans. An income tax was instituted and there was opening discussion of enacting *social insurance* (Social Security) such as Germany had created back in 1884. The Progressives were calling on the federal government to assume more active responsibility on social issues. The government's response was largely positive and broad-based enough to significantly expand human services across its subsystems.

Until 1917, when the United States entered World War I, the Progressive reformers had spurred Americans and their government to take action in supporting human services development with unprecedented force. The reforms were wide-ranging and permanent. Americans were receptive to bringing changes to society which would truly make the United States the "land of equal opportunity." A number of factors—the growth of labor unions; restraints on business interests; government acknowledgement of increased responsibility for the quality of life; technological and medical advancements— reinforced a general commitment to improving the standard of living for *every* American citizen. The subsequent enactment of legislative safeguards protecting people's rights all bear witness to society's progressive attitude towards emerging human services issues.

The first twenty years of this century have also been referred to as the *sociological era* in America. During this time, an awareness grew markedly among Americans of the interplay between various societal forces which influence the quality of life. The belief in any "single causation" of social or personal problems diminished as explanations of the apparent inequalities and inconsistencies which existed in American life. As the evidence piled up, people had to accept the fact that the need for more human services had nothing to do with an individual's inadequacy. Rather, the need was created by the individual's society. As society cast a more critical eye on its economic structure—and the inequality perpetuated by the economy—it was able to realize that the old Social Darwinist answer to the existence of human need was certainly very illogical. The economy, operating "automatically" as the laissez-faire fans wished was still of great benefit to the Haves. But, without external regulation of the economy, there was no accounting for the negative effects of unbridled profit motives on the lives of the still-present Have-nots. From a sociological perspective, Americans came to see that human need wasn't rooted in any "moral flaw" of the individual, but in a flawed economy that perpetuated a society of Haves and Have-nots and maintained an imbalance in income distribution throughout the country.

As America entered the "Roaring Twenties," the country had proven itself to be a world power to be reckoned with and was emerging further as a nation of unparalleled affluence. If all the Americans were not sharing the wealth, at least America was beginning to see a connection between economics and the delivery of adequate human services . . . and was beginning to do something about it.

The twenties were a time of continuing prosperity and an era in which society began to implement the legislation for expanded human services which had been fought for and won by the Progressives. Prevention of deprivation, however, was no longer a national priority. Fortunately, significant changes had been successfully wrought during the relatively short period that had earlier concerned itself with

"What is helpful?". World War I seems to have effectively altered American consciousness once more. During the twenties, people's self-interest again replaced their sense of community spirit and commitment to human services. People almost abruptly turned away from concentrating on the "common good" and issues relating to social justice and equality. Instead, they took up a decided preoccupation with themselves as individuals.

How is this new shift in national attitudes and interests to be explained this time? To be sure, the experience of participating in a world war had an impact and promoted a turning-inward among most Americans. Their pronounced movement in this direction is probably, however, more directly attributable to the emergence of Ford and Freud as folk heroes. These two men—Henry Ford and Sigmund Freud—have, without a doubt, been the two most influential men of the twentieth century. Together, their work and their orientations have shaped American attitudes and thought since their zenith in the twenties.

Henry Ford was the founding father of modern, super-industrialized America. Ford represented many things: money; social mobility; and, above all, materialism. Americans in the 1920s—and since—have not yet ceased to be all but overcome by the endless procession of material goods available in this country of ours. After the Progressive Era, it wasn't that Americans wanted to undo their reforms. They just lost interest in them. The glitter of wealth and all it

Sigmund Freud.   *Henry Ford.*

could buy held more fascination than any prolonged attention to righting further social wrongs. Hollywood had been created. Industrialization hadn't slackened its pace. The "flappers" wanted only the fantasies and goodies society was generating. Their attention span for more serious concerns had apparently become exceedingly short.

The continuing availability of more and more material goods to more and more people seems to have created the "cycle of rising expectations" (discussed earlier). The more people got, the more they wanted. The old laissez-faire economists may have been very happy with this cycle, as big business undoubtedly was, but such rampant acquisitiveness was not without consequences. The twenties were to end disastrously.

Before they did, however, another seed was planted that would continue to grow in American thinking right up to the present day. This was the work of Sigmund Freud. Although this psychoanalyst was an Austrain who only visited the United States once, his impact on American thinking has been quite profound. He might be likened to a latter-day John Calvin, in a way. Freud introduced a number of psychoanalytic concepts that returned the individual to center stage and left the influence of the environment on the sidelines. While the earlier 1900s had been the "sociological era," the years from 1920 to at least 1960 are aptly referred to as the *psychological era*. Instead of trying to analyze environmental forces, people sought to gain insight into their own psyches, to know about the effects of their "formative years," to understand themselves more completely. People began to lean toward a new viewpoint. Namely, they began to speculate that human problems might be rooted not so much in inequality and environmental difficulties as in individuals' own "hang-ups." Sound familiar?

By this time, you're probably wondering if society will ever remain loyal to one point of view about people, helpfulness, or the delivery of human services. That is seriously doubtful! Toward the end of the twenties, people's attitudes had shifted significantly backward. Although the psychology mania of the twenties was not exactly the same as the Calvinistic doctrine which ascribed human problems to a "moral flaw" in the individual; nevertheless, the two philosophies would probably have agreed that a person's failure to function effectively in a society was surely due to some inadequacy within the individual, whether it was labeled sin or intrapsychic conflict. This common ground between the two social theories could have pushed society perilously close to a renewed faith in Social Darwinism on a large scale, if other events had not intervened. Bearing that danger in mind, what happened to American society next may well have been, after all, a blessing in disguise—in very good disguise. On October 24, 1929, the bottom fell out: the stock market crashed!

Just the year before, President Hoover, in an address to the nation, had congratulated Americans on wiping out deprivation from their incredibly prosperous land. History has, of course, proven those remarks to be rather premature. The Crash in '29 was the result of thoughtless, planless economic maneuvering by business interests who foresaw no limits to the profits possible in the market place. But, there were limits. A greedy imbalance between supply and demand had been brought to the breaking point by a basically unhealthy and unregulated economy. People endlessly wanted more. Business endlessly wanted more. Something had to give; the economy had to collapse. It could no longer pull its own weight.

From glorious, gold-trimmed affluence, America fell into a deep, despondent Depression from which it would take no less than six years to even begin to rally. If people were beginning to blame themselves, or more specifically the Have-nots, for their own deprivation again, they were cut short by the rapid, seemingly unavoidable swelling of the Have-nots' ranks and the mushrooming need for the most basic and essential human services for survival. In 1930, four million Americans were unemployed. Their numbers doubled in one year. By November 1932, when Franklin Delano Roosevelt was elected to the presidency, there were fifteen million Americans out of work. This time no one mistook the unemployment rosters for evidence of a "moral flaw" or believed that the need for expanded basic human services reflected "personal failure."

Roosevelt sought to encourage Americans and to restore the economy by creating a package of human services programs called the New Deal. Urging everyone on with his conviction, "We have nothing to fear but fear itself," FDR attacked the Depression by making work available for as many people as possible and by providing direct assistance for those who were in need, but unemployable. America was in a severe crisis. In some parts of the country, at least 40% of the people were receiving assistance while in other rural areas almost 90% of the residents could not survive without help. The government gradually realized that private philanthropic organizations didn't have the funds or the capacity to provide sufficient human services—particularly money—to the overwhelming numbers of Americans who were being victimized by the out-of-control economy. It was imperative that the government step in and develop new solutions to protect its people and provide them with adequate human services, quickly and effectively.

Social Security

On August 14, 1935, the government made into law the *Social Security Act*—a monumental movement by the federal government to take responsibility for and to provide essential human services directly to the American people. This historic legislation reaffirmed Americans' *right* to security from the instability of economic forces and was insurance against future deprivation of their basic human needs because of the unpredictability of the market place and life, in general.

A thorough analysis of the Social Security Act is beyond the scope of this text, but it is recommended to every student of human services, nonetheless. Social Security contributed a great deal toward protecting Americans from external economic threats, although perhaps not far enough toward preventing the repetition of the damage that unregulated business interests had brought. Despite its shortcomings, however, the Social Security Act is a landmark in human services legislation and people-oriented policy-making.

The Social Security Act is comprised of three major components:

I   *Social Insurance Programs*
   - old age insurance
   - unemployment compensation

II   *Public Assistance Programs*
   - Old Age Assistance
   - Aid to the Blind
   - Aid to Dependent Children
   - Aid to the Disabled (added in 1950)

III   *Health and Welfare Services*
   - maternal and child health
   - crippled children
   - child welfare
   - vocational rehabilitation
   - public health

The original Social Security Act has been periodically amended by Congress over the years since its inception to increase the numbers of Americans eligible for the various human services benefits it encompasses. There has also been a steady enlargement of the areas of federal support for health and welfare programs being made available to Americans. This continual expansion of social insurance provisions bears witness to the fact that twentieth century America has come to believe that society, through its government, has a clear responsibility for insuring the well-being of all its people, Haves and Have-nots alike, through the adequate provision of human services. The present levels of insurance and services are by no means overly generous or even entirely adequate. However, they are an encouragement that the needs of the many do count over the self-interest of a few in the United States. Such a new national attitude put to rest the old faith in laissez faire; the trust in the merits of an uncontrolled market place; and the myth of personal independence or self-sufficiency in modern society. Instead, there has been a growing awareness that economic forces and social systems must be harnessed and guided to serve people better.

Earlier it was stated, somewhat facetiously, that the Depression may have been a blessing in good disguise. Of course, none of us would ever call the misery of millions during those years any kind of blessing. But, society's response to the Depression and its strengthened commitment to human services afterwards were certainly of significant benefit to all of us—and will continue to be in the future.

MID-CENTURY

We know that old social attitudes tend to be persistent and sometimes never change entirely. By the 1940s, there was already a good deal of criticism about the "Welfare State" that FDR had created through the Social Security Act some years earlier. (For some reason, the United States is probably the only place where "welfare" is a dirty word.) With their usual short memories, many American people had forgotten that before the 1935 legislation, an estimated 42% of the population had to share no more than 1% of the total population's income. Once the crisis of the Depression was past and Americans were getting back to "business as usual," some of them returned to their old, rather self-serving attitudes about helpfulness; about human services; and about the Have-nots. But, there really was no going back for American society.

The foundation of the human services profession had been laid and could not be easily dislodged. Beginning as the century was born and solidified during the Depression, the philosophy of the human services profession had crystallized by the 1940s and would not be undone. By then, professionals across the human services disciplines were reaching several conclusions simultaneously:

- **People had the right to expect their society, through its technology and other resources, to prevent their deprivation and provide for their basic human needs.**
- **The society, through its government, had the irrevocable responsibility for providing people with adequate human services.**
- **Meeting people's needs comprehensively and effectively required an understanding of the "whole person" and his relationship to his environment.**
- **Meeting the "whole person's" needs meant that the resources of many disciplines should be cooperatively mobilized for him.**

There was, indeed, no going back for human services or for society. The Depression had proven that people were interdependent and that society should be guided more by people-motives than by the profit-motive in years to come.

Universal vs. Residual Services

Some controversies around "What is helpful?" did continue, of course. Most Americans had resolved by then that such services as social security and free education along with public services, such as parks, libraries, and highways, to name just a few, were everyone's right in the United States. Other services, such as public assistance and national health insurance were considered quite different matters, however. Most Americans, to this day, are still highly ambivalent about the provision of these human services in anything resembling adequate amounts. Such controversies will go on because, as we know, there are no permanent answers to "What is helpful?" and there is never a unanimous answer in a country as large as the United States.

Traditionally, human services have been divided into two types:

1   • *universal* (sometimes called *institutional*)

        and

2   • *residual*

A *universal service* is one that is accessible to every member of society by virtue of citizenship alone. Public school education and public libraries are two examples of such services. On the other hand, a *residual service* is accessible to only certain segments of the population. For example, Medicaid is available only to the poor or elderly. Graduate school education is generally only accessible to those who can pay. While it is clear that some services should, according to our democratic precepts, remain residual while others should be universal, there is a great deal of controversy over which should be which. There is a growing movement among human services professionals and the general citizenry to increase the scope of universal services for every American. For example, the instituting of national health insurance and the development of sufficient day care services are thought by many to be essential human services of which no individual or family should be deprived because of income level. The human services profession takes the position that every American is entitled to whatever services are needed to promote his well-being. Present-day society, however, will decide whether providing such services as national health insurance or day care is "helpful" to individuals and to the general society. As you can see, there have always been new considerations when answering the question, "What is helpful?" over the years, and it is likely that this will always be true.

By 1945, the United States had brought on the Atomic Age by mercilessly and perhaps needlessly unleashing the bomb on unsuspecting Hiroshima. The prosperity that followed the end of World War II raised new issues around "What is helpful?" and encouraged the further development of human services. America's economic and industrial forces had geared up for World War II and emerged after it convinced that FDR's New Deal had put human services scarcity in the past tense.

In the 1950s, Americans were once again reaping the material rewards of an affluent economy unmatched anywhere else in the world. As was their custom, the Haves were once again enjoying themselves in rather blissful ignorance of the continuing plight of the Have-nots. The access to human services was still far from equal for all Americans. Most alarming of all the inequities in human services was the continuing spectre of poverty in America. It would appear that America has almost a chronic case of *social blindness* when it comes to viewing the realities of inequality. It is one of the ironies of industrialization that even the poorest people can look well-dressed. Except in the most extreme situations, even those with the least can buy clothing to imitate a "success wardrobe." It is, of course, even easier to disguise the unavailability of adequate educational, medical, mental health, or other human services.

Whether visible or not, the fact remains that by 1960, only two-thirds of the American people were not victims of continuing economic and social deprivation. Over 40 million Americans were! Given the total U.S. population then, a solid 25% of Americans were Have-nots, living at the poverty line.[1] That meant that in addition to being without money, all those people were surely without all the other services needed to increase their healthiness, improve their literacy, and enhance their mental and social stability.

Whether Americans were willing to admit it or not, inequality and a consequent inequitable distribution of human services were very much the case by the end of the 1950s. There remained millions of Have-nots without access to services to meet their needs. Who are the twentieth-century Have-nots anyway? They are, as they have always been, the "leftovers" of industrial society: the aged; the disabled; the children; the unskilled laborers; members of minority groups; and all the other people labeled as failures because of their inability to hold their own in the market place. If you remember, using a person's market-place productivity to measure his worth is not exactly a new idea. But, it is obviously an idea with a long life!

The 1960s brought, fortunately, a new perspective to society's thinking about Haves and Have-nots and also a further solidification of the human services philosophy. This was the era of the Civil Rights Movement and the War on Poverty. It would be wishful thinking to

---

[1]The "poverty line" in 1976 was set at an income of $5,500 for an urban family of four. Twenty years ago it was far less.

The Have-Nots.

state that either one of these monumental efforts on behalf of equality and social justice were all-out successes. In retrospect, we can see that racism still exists pervasively in the United States and that meaningful income redistribution that would truly eradicate poverty is far from achieved. Some very significant gains were made, however, by these two efforts toward insuring more equal access to human services. Also, more of society's resources were made available for the expansion of human services to larger numbers of Americans of all races and social classes.

The Civil Rights Movement did increase the educational, social, and occupational opportunities of the nation's minorities. It did not succeed in achieving an end to discrimination and prejudice, which are lodged so deeply in America's thinking. But, a strong beginning was made upon which the human services profession must now build. Likewise, though the War on Poverty is criticized as nothing more than a minor skirmish, it did bring some results. It decreased the percentage of Have-nots from 25% to 12% in a few years. This was surely an accomplishment—even if one recalls that 12% also represented the number of Have-nots way back in 1904. During its active years, a number of federally sponsored programs were created to attack the environmental roots of inequality—unequal employment, urban decay, and inadequate schooling. Clearly, the programs were still geared mostly toward making fundamental inequality more tolerable—not unlike helping efforts of earlier centuries. There was a big difference, however. That difference was the emerging human services profession.

TODAY AND TOMORROW

Throughout this analysis of the history of human services, we have looked at two trends simultaneously

- **the existence (and persistence) of poverty; and**
- **the expansion of accessible human services to more and more people in American society.**

It would have been a crucial mistake, I believe, to look at the developments in society which favored the growth of human services without also looking at the ever-present reality of poverty in this country. Standing alone, the mushrooming of human services, particularly in the twentieth century, speaks as evidence of society's strong commitment to the needs of its people. However, when one looks at the broader picture and sees that millions of people are *still* poor and otherwise deprived, it should become clear to the reader that human services has a lot of work to do!

America of the 1970s has not realized its founding fathers' dreams about "equality" yet. Nor has it fully implemented the guidelines set down by the Progressives earlier in this century. We could—and many social philosophers surely will—devote countless hours and essays to analyzing the whys and wherefores of the persistence of a class of Have-nots in a productive society where it's now so unnecessary for deprivation to continue. We *must* look for the answers to the riddles of the past if we are to avert the tendency of history to repeat itself in the field of human services. Human services has learned to look neither to psychology nor to sociology exclusively for the answers to social problems, inequality, or human needs. Rather, we must anticipate finding the answers in a clearer understanding of the interplay between the whole person and his society. We know that we must constantly be asking and then asking again that old question, "What is helpful?" And we must be willing to act effectively on the answers we find.

A Human Services Perspective

The human services worker has to ask the "What is helpful?" question both of individuals and of the society or community, acknowledging the interdependence of the two. For example, if the worker finds that conditions in the society aren't healthy, how can the society produce healthy individuals? And, if individuals are often unhealthy, then it follows that their society must be unwell, too. Struggling to better understand why today's society with all its potential has so many shortcomings in providing for its people is a paramount task for human services. Why, for example, has there been a continuing attitude among the Haves that the Have-nots should "pull themselves up by their bootstraps"? Didn't they notice that the Have-nots were barefoot?

Human services must paint on a very broad canvas. Society really hasn't done that before. Without a duly broad interpretation of the societal attitudes that shape people's lives and the human services available to them, we will never adequately understand "What is helpful?" or be able to do anything about it.

By broadening its scope, human services has been able to see more clearly the mistakes of earlier periods in history. It must now try to unravel the mixed-up social doctrines and traditional practices that have become obstacles to the adequate delivery of comprehensive human services and the obliteration of inequality. The history of human services in the United States and in Europe, upon review, seems a chronology of half-measures and woefully inadequate solutions to peoples' needs and to problems that wouldn't go away over hundreds of years.

The human services philosophy has grown out of an attempt to assess the unsuccessful efforts in the past to help people and to improve the quality of life. Implementing that philosophy and achieving the goals of the human services profession will depend on the profession's ability to utilize the knowledge of the past and to anticipate the needs of the future. We are now in a *Transitional Age*, a time when not many of society's time-honored values and directions are being embraced without question. Those of us who remain committed to human services—with the full knowledge of the double-barrelled implications of the inadequacies of the past and the unpredictability of the future—most definitely have our work cut out for us.

We know that, after thousands of years, inequality is still alive and well in our midst. We know, too, that in order to eliminate inequality and provide truly equitable and adequate human services to *all* the people in our society, we must challenge the society's fundamental assumptions about Haves and Have-nots. We must remember to ask, today and tomorrow, "What *is* helpful?" and we must be able to deliver an array of adequate and comprehensive services that really are helpful.

BIBLIOGRAPHY

De Schweinitz, Karl. *England's Road to Social Security*. New York: A.S. Barnes and Co., 1961.

Galbraith, John Kenneth. *The Affluent Society*. New York: Houghton Mifflin, 1958.

Harrington, Michael. *The Other America*. New York: Random House, 1962.

Leuchtenberg, William E. *The Perils of Prosperity: 1914–1932*. Chicago: University of Chicago Press, 1958.

Manchester, William. *The Glory and the Dream*. Vols. 1, 2. Boston: Little, Brown and Co., 1973.

New York Times. October 6, 1974.

Piven, Frances Fox and Cloward, Richard. *Regulating the Poor*. New York: Macmillan, 1971.

Reich, Charles A. *The Greening of America*. New York: Random House, 1970.

Weinberger, Paul E. *Perspectives on Social Welfare*. New York: Macmillan, 1969.

Wilensky, Harold L. and Libeaux, Charles N. *Industrial Society and the Welfare State*. New York: Russell Sage Foundation, 1958.

chapter four

Social Policy and Planning

The human services didn't "just happen." Society created the policy and developed the plans that brought it into existence. As a review of human services history has shown, social policy has a significant influence on people in a society and on their interrelationships. It is, therefore, important that human services workers have a clear understanding of social policy in the United States as it effects their own lives and their ability to help other people.

WHAT IS SOCIAL POLICY?

Every society, through its lawmakers, creates policies to spell out how it will deal with its major concerns. These include: foreign policy, economic policy, political policy, and social policy. In the United States, Congress is empowered by the people to decide what the American attitude will be to other nations of the world; how the economy should best be regulated; what measures may be needed to protect the democratic political system created by the Constitution; and what kind of relationship the government will have with its people and their needs.

Social policy (sometimes called domestic policy) is really a blueprint of society's social goals and priorities, based on the society's dominant values and beliefs and is, therefore, a key to understanding what makes society tick. Social policy outlines the principles governing the society's actions towards achieving its social goals and solving its social problems. Through its social policy, a society defines which areas of human needs the society itself is responsible for meeting and which needs shall be left to the individual to fill for himself. In the U.S., for example, social policy determines that free public school

69

education must be provided for every youngster. College education, however, is not interpreted by social policy as society's responsibility.

A society's social policy is not always entirely beneficial. It can promote the meeting of human needs, but it can also be designed to prevent it. Social policy is an expression of the will of the people, but it isn't always representative of the needs and interests of *all* the people in the society. South Africa's apartheid, Hitler's Germany, and the past practice of slavery and current realities of racism in the United States are all examples of social policy which was not beneficial to all the people. Most, societies, however (including our own), have developed social policies that are of at least some benefit to all members. In fact, every modern industrialized society has now adopted social policies to promote the meeting of people's health, education, and welfare needs.

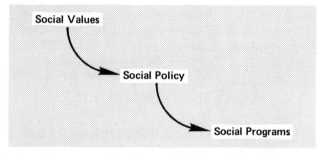

In every society, social policy mirrors the society's values in interaction with other societal forces, such as: cultural and religious traditions, available resources, the level of technology, the political system, and the state of the economy. Social policy is probably most closely related to economic policy. It becomes a chicken-or-egg question to ask which comes first or which is most important. Historically, both have been so closely intertwined that it is almost impossible to tell. The sociologist Max Weber gives one example of this close interrelationship by noting that capitalism and the Protestant ethic couldn't have gotten very far without each other. If people hadn't placed great value on hard work and achievement, there wouldn't have been a labor force to support the factory system that was the backbone of capitalistic economics. Even today, we see how closely people are linked to the market place. For many generations now, profit-motives have been of greater interest to the society than people-motives.

It seems to generally hold true that social values and economic values must complement and reinforce each other. When they do not, society's stability is unhinged by the conflict. Very fundamental changes in either or both sets of values will then be required if the society is to go on functioning. Such a change in values usually means that a change in the character of the society will not be far behind. America, after its 1929 Stock Market Crash is evidence of this. Until then economic values really had the upper hand. However, the enormous human misery that resulted brought an end to such unregulated economic activity and a beginning to a social policy that placed more importance on people than on profits. America emerged from that crisis with a new character—a society firmly committed to promoting income security for everyone, through government involvement in the economy. Had not the society's battling values been successfully realigned, it is hard to guess what shape the country might now be in.

Social policy requires making many economic decisions about the use and distribution of society's resources—its money, materials, and manpower—to meet people's needs. Social policy determines which and how much of those resources are to be earmarked for the development of programs and the creation of services to meet human needs. Obviously, when a society takes wide responsibility for meeting its members' needs, the social policy it generates will direct proportionally high expenditures of resources for meeting needs. If, on the other hand, a society either has different values that don't emphasize people motives or is incapable, because of limited resources, of meeting needs, the resulting social policy is likely to reflect society's conviction in the importance of every individual's self-sufficiency.

As pictured in the chart below, social values set a process in motion which ultimately either leads to or decides against the development and support of the social programs comprising the human services.

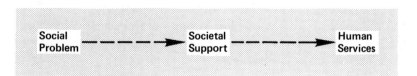

When a social problem has been identified, the society's values will determine how it is to be solved and will initiate social policy based on that decision. If society itself takes responsibility for solving the problem, policy (and enabling legislation, if needed) will be made to permit the use of fiscal and/or other resources for developing whichever service may be needed to solve the problem.

Although social values are pivotal to the formulation of social policy, those values are not always clear-cut. Values aren't necessarily constant or stable or harmonious. They are rarely eternal and sometimes not even equally accepted in different sectors of the society. Not all values are conscious or explicit either. Often, in fact, values do contradict each other and change significantly over time. Some of the conflicting values commonly effecting social policy (and life in general) are:

cooperation	vs.	competition
group interests	vs.	individual interests
security	vs.	humanitarianism
independence	vs.	interdependence
enjoyment	vs.	endurance
stability	vs.	change
status quo	vs.	growth
rationality	vs.	feelings
justice	vs.	charity
tradition	vs.	innovation
compassion	vs.	control

When a society's values are in conflict or in the process of changing, its social policy will understandably be inconsistent. Reviewing the historical development of the human services shows clearly that such value battles and transformations have happened in our own society more than once. At various stages during its growth, American society has held different values in prominence and has developed accompanying social policies based on them. As values changed, so did policy. For example, when America's founding fathers stated that "all men are created equal," they were outlining Colonial social policy and providing us with a good clue to some of the social values of their times. Of course, the men they referred to were strictly the landowners of the time. Other men, who didn't own property were excluded. Black men were slaves then and not even considered human. And, the equality of women surely crossed nobody's mind!

Social values have thankfully changed and things are a little better today.

Social Costs

While many of us may believe that American social policy *still* isn't encompassing enough to adequately meet every American's needs, we must all agree that history shows a steady increase in government responsibility and involvement toward solving social problems and meeting the needs of all U.S. citizens. As the family and the private market have become less and less able to provide sufficiently for people's needs, the government has stepped in to fill the gap. The government has been increasingly willing to do this because it has learned the *social costs* of unmet human needs. In other words, society has become aware that when some of its members are deprived of equal opportunity for health, housing, education, and other life-supporting services, it is not only that person or his family who suffers. The whole society is also damaged. When some of us must live in slums, or receive inferior education, or survive on nutritionally low diets, or have no help to turn to for relief of mental disturbances, all of us are diminished. Great attention has been given in recent years to ecology and the importance of stopping pollution before it makes our planet uninhabitable. Human ecology stresses the similar importance of making a just society which can sustain healthy human beings. America knows now that it cannot afford the social costs which result from ignoring people and widespread social problems. Contemporary social policy indicates a broadening sense of concern and responsibility in society for eradicating the social problems and inequities that carry such devastatingly high social costs.

To be sure, the road ahead isn't entirely smooth. There remain some conflicts in society's values which will continue to make social policy somewhat inconsistent. Nevertheless, let us hope that the revolution of rising expectations will continue and prompt even greater demand for people-centered human services.

HUMAN SERVICES POLICY

The philosophy of human services is grounded in a commitment to enhancing the lives of each member of American society by providing equal opportunity to everyone for the assurance of adequate income, nutrition, education, housing, health, and mental health services as well as other life-supporting services which will enable people to lead satisfying lives together in a just society.

Historically, American social policy has been remedial and reactive. That is, policy has been developed to deal with a social problem only after the problem already exists and has grown to big enough proportions to gain attention and cause alarm. (Sort of like locking the barn after the horse was stolen.) Human services policy which will, hopefully, be adopted as America's social policy for the future will take another approach. In a sense, it will "go looking for trouble." Policy will dictate *prevention* as a social goal. The aim of social programs will be expanded to include the provision of whatever services may be needed to prevent the occurrence of those conditions in society which are injurious to its members' good functioning and well-being. This new emphasis on prevention is already evident throughout the human services subsystems. Some notable examples are: In the health field, treating a child for lead poisoning is not enough. It is also essential to prevent an epidemic of lead poisoning by attacking existing environmental conditions that encourage it. In the corrections field, punishment without rehabilitation is inadequate and prevention of criminality at its roots also needs to be addressed. In child welfare, youngsters are not to be moved into foster care until every possible effort has been made to prevent family breakdown. Countless comparable examples can be drawn from the other subsystems as well to highlight the human services thrust towards prevention.

The values inherent in the human services philosophy provide the framework for **Human Services Policy** which is designed to:

- **Build a just society in which every member has the opportunity and the right to meet his human needs**

- **Create services that are adequately responsive to meeting people's needs and functionally able to provide for those needs**

- **Prevent conditions in society which threaten or interfere with meeting people's needs or enabling them to live satisfying lives**

- **Develop an integrated network of human services which can meet the needs of the whole person through the optimal use of society's resources**

- **Maintain services that are accountable to the consumer and relevant to solving people's problems**

In all its efforts, human services policy will emphasize the importance of making systems work for people. In doing so, America will take a giant step towards insuring a socially healthy future.

SOCIAL PLANNING FOR HUMAN SERVICES

Social planning is the "how-to" piece of society's problem-solving. Planning is the means of putting policy into action. The United States has not always been as planful as it should have been. There seems to have been a tendency to plan too little too late—particularly in the human services. The mistake of waiting for tomorrow's problems to take care of themselves has been painfully pointed out by the enormous social costs this neglect has brought. Also, we now know that our natural resources are not unlimited as we once thought they were. In our turbulent and transitional times, it is beginning to appear that if we don't soon learn to plan wisely for the future, our mushrooming social problems will far outrun our capacity to solve them.

Putting human services theory into practice is urgently needed. However, doing so is not an easy job—and definitely not a quick one! A great deal of painstaking planning is involved. Since World War II there has been an incredible increase in the demand for human services and a proliferation of them. Current social policy permits the expenditure of fully one-third of the GNP (Gross National Product) for the provision of health, mental health, education, welfare, recreation, and other human services. This expanded meeting of people's needs has undoubtedly solved a lot of social problems. Unfortunately, solving one problem sometimes can create another.

Solving a problem in a hurry can also sometimes have undesired long-term consequences. For example, although billions of dollars are now made available for human services, it is not necessarily true that all that money is wisely spent. And, it is not unthinkable that the hugely increased expenditures may be spent mostly for "more of the same" traditional services delivered in the same old-fashioned, fragmented ways. It is highly doubtful that the needs of the whole person are being any better met now. What is needed is an integration of services designed to respond to the needs of the whole person. Achieving this requires level-headed, cooperative planning.

The Planning Process

To be of maximum benefit to the whole person, human services must be:

- **coordinated and integrated**
- **accessible and comprehensive**
- **effective and efficient**

Planning services to incorporate those characteristics cannot be random or haphazard or even spontaneous. Instead, all human services planning must follow a clearly defined process with a number of essential and sequential steps. This *Planning Process* is:

1 • **Identify the problem**

2 • **Set goals; establish priorities**

3 • **Gather data; assess alternatives**

4 • **Develop a program**

5 • **Evaluate the program**

Whether discussing the implementation of Human Services Policy itself or some development within a subsystem, the planning process will be the same. To further illustrate the process, let's assume that we are interested in realigning a city's traditionally separate human services into a meaningful and comprehensive *network*. This might be called "human services bridge-building" and must be achieved by carrying out the steps of the planning process in proper sequence. The work would probably look something like this:

1 • *Problem Identification* • A city-wide conference is held at which the leaders of various health, welfare, and other human services agree that their traditional ways of providing for people's needs are not necessarily giving the best results. Discussion leads them to conclude that there is, indeed, a significant problem because a) the needs of the whole person are not being met and b) the available resources are not being used in ways that will bring the most benefits to the most people.

2 • Goal-setting • Having defined the problem as the inadequacy of traditional patterns of service delivery, the participants in the discussion are able to agree next on the goal to resolve their mutual problem. They decide to sponsor efforts aimed at coordinating and integrating their services in a more relevant way, by creating a human services network.

Goal setting here hasn't been happening in a vacuum. There has been attention given to "sizing up the situation" confronting them and to understanding their total city environment with all its salient social, political, and economic realities. "Wishful thinking" goals are quickly abandoned and the cooperation and collaboration of the leaders (who are both consumers and providers of services) focus on defining goals which are considered achievable.

When the major goal (creating a network) has been set, the group moves on to establishing priorities for the other related goals. In this example, the group must address itself to giving priority to the components of the network—*coordination, integration, accessibility, comprehensiveness, efficiency, and effectiveness.* The group will rank each of these characteristics according to the relative importance they agree each should have in the creation of the network. The group may decide that the first task and highest priority should be given to making sure that all the services are equally accessible to all the people in the city who could use them. Once that is achieved, the next priority might go to coordination and the development of linkages with open channels of communication between systems. And so on until all priorities are established.

3 • Data-gathering • Once the problem is understood, goals set, and priorities established, it is time for the group to outline as fully as possible what the obstacles are that might stand in the way of solving the problem. Facts must also be gathered about the resources available to the group for use in reaching the goal.

For human services bridge-building, the fact finding phase should turn up a good deal of information about the existing boundaries between systems and the ways in which they might be short-circuiting service delivery. There are usually three conditions created by old service arrangements that have a particularly negative effect on efforts to help the whole person. These are: *duplication, fragmentation*, and *specialization*. The group, in close and honest self-scrutiny is almost certain to find these conditions present among their systems. The various helping systems when arranged in traditional patterns have tended to duplicate each others' efforts much of the time. Also, because the systems tend to "guard their turf" and maintain a veil of secrecy, there is little of the needed communication that would help their efforts from being fragmented. To make matters worse, each system of the old style has become increasingly specialized in the kind of help it offers and, therefore, has proportionally diminished the number of people it can really help. Obviously, these three, interrelated conditions make it virtually impossible for the whole person to find adequate and relevant help and are, therefore, obstacles to be overcome by planning.

4 • Program Development • Once the facts were in, the information had to be weighed and some decisions reached about the most feasible way to proceed to reach the planning goal. The group in this example saw only two alternatives open to them—either they could abandon their old ways of doing things altogether, or they could use as many of the existing services as possible with the introduction of human service-oriented modifications. The temptation to "start from scratch" in planning services is always an enticing one, but hardly realistic. The radical change implied by the first alternative would have been chaotic and surely created more problems than it solved. The second alternative, therefore, was the most sound: to modify existing service patterns in such a way as to make them more capable of meeting the needs of the whole person. To achieve this, the leaders set in motion activities in each of their systems which would quickly open the channels of communication among them. In this way, *linkages* were established and a newly-created human services network was on its way.

When the groundwork has been solidly laid and the planning process has been faithfully followed, the actual task of turning theory into practice is invariably made simpler. Asking the right question and gathering enough facts make it possible to successfully reach planning goals. When the planning fails, it is usually because the goals were too ambiguous in the first place or there was a serious gap in the information used to put together a meaningful program. Planning seeks to make optimal use of knowledge, people, and resources.

Doing so is only possible when every appropriate step along the way to program development is well taken.

5 • *Evaluation* • The development of a program should not mark the end of planning. In fact, in the human services it is accurate to say that planning is really never completely finished. Just the opposite! Because times change and people's needs change along with them, there's never an occasion to rest on one's laurels in human services. Right now we're very critical of traditional service patterns and the inadequacies in them. However, there was a time when people were satisfied with them. And, there might come a time when people grow just as discontented with the programs being created now. We've agreed that we cannot solve today's problems with yesterday's solutions. So what makes us think that today's solutions will be welcome and helpful for tomorrow's problems?

Hopefully, the group in our example did not just initiate a network of services and then forget about it. Rather, they should have agreed to share the monitoring of the network's functioning and jointly evaluate, on an ongoing basis, the effectiveness of the network. Their evaluation efforts should focus on five factors:

- **effort**
- **performance**
- **impact**
- **efficiency**
- **process**

Together they should determine whether or not sufficient (or excessive) effort was being taken to maintain the network. Then they should judge whether the network is really increasing the effectiveness of service delivery to the consumer and whether it is doing so in the most efficient manner. There are many evaluation questions they might ask—Is the network linking people with systems?—Does the network make services readily accessible to everyone?—Is continuity of service built into the network?—Are the services linkages maintaining open channels of communication and sharing information?—Are the services being provided of the same good quality for every consumer?—Are the services really meeting the whole person's needs?

The likelihood of creating a perfect network is about as remote as creating a perfect society. That's why evaluation is so important and why it must be ongoing. Perfection may not be possible, but there's no reason not to keep a watchful eye on the network to make sure it's doing its imperfect best at all times to link systems and people in the most beneficial way for every consumer of human services.

Evaluation serves another purpose, too. As was noted earlier, asking the right questions is imperative for successful planning. Questions are also needed to stimulate relevant research in human services that will enable us to anticipate and predict more accurately and more fully what people's needs will be and what will be most helpful to meeting those needs as we gallop into the future. By the evaluation of current human services networks and programs, we should be able to cite critical indicators of meaningful, satisfying, productive community lives.

RESEARCH IN THE HUMAN SERVICES

The research in the human services has been woefully inadequate and in short supply. With the possible exception of the health field, there has generally been far too little time or effort devoted to relevant research. Maybe that's because people who like working with other people tend to feel uncomfortable around computers and calculators and such. That's not just a shame. It could become very detrimental to everybody!

Human services workers must learn to ask "Why?" and to search for answers in every aspect of their work. We can't be satisfied with only solving the immediate problem at hand. We have to ask why the problem came into existence in the first place. The questions are endless: Why can't Johnny read? Why is the school system producing thousands of high school graduates who can't read? Why does Barbara steal? Why are so many senior citizens malnourished? Why do so many patients in mental hospitals receive only custodial care? Why does Martha neglect her children? Why are 12% of Americans living below the "poverty line," subsisting on less than $5,038 a year?

There are just as many "How?" questions: How can Johnny and his classmates receive relevant reading instruction? How can Barbara be helped? How can adequate and innovative nutritional services be distributed to the elderly? How can community-based psychiatry programs get more support? How can Martha find counseling for herself and day care for her children? How can the incongruence of "Poverty in Plenty" be wiped out once and for all in the United States?

Answering these questions and all the others that face human services will require that we ask the right questions and then put our technology to work for us to find the answers. We need to learn a great deal more about people and their needs and about what is truly helpful. We also need to learn a great deal more about how social policy is made and how it can be influenced. We also need to learn more about what is needed for the most effective social planning. Forewarned *is* forearmed. Raising the level of our research competence can warn us in time of the conditions which threaten the quality of life. Knowing this can rally us to prevent the threat from having any impact in reality.

Research will also be needed to guide us in making the best possible use of our resources in the future. Research can be used to measure the *cost–benefits* of the services we provide in order to tell us whether the relationship between the kind and quality of service and the cost of the service is a reasonable and positive one which makes best use of resources.

We know that we live in changing times and that changes in our society are going to continue to occur in coming decades and even longer. We, therefore, must make use of whatever research techniques and skills are at our disposal to systematically assess what we are doing, the way in which we are doing it, and what we will need to be doing in the future. It is precisely because traditional service patterns neglected to do their homework in researching and evaluating their efforts, that their services became less and less responsive to the needs of the whole person. Clearly, if the same mistake is to be avoided by human services, a commitment to ongoing research and evaluation has to be made and kept by all of us in the profession.

HUMAN SERVICES MODULES

Human services organizations in all the subsystems share certain characteristics in common which are bound together by human services philosophy and policy. *First*, a human service organization is not profit-motivated. The organization—whether it be a clinic, school, hospital, or agency—has not been established for the purpose of making money for its creators. It has been designed instead to provide service and to use whatever money is available to provide more and better service. Organizations must, of course, be concerned about finances in order to survive, but their financial interests are focused on "breaking even" so that they can pay salaries, rents, and so on. They are not interested in making a profit on the services they provide. *Second*, a human service organization places primary importance on satisfying the consumer, not the producer. Unlike profit-making organizations in which the interest in pleasing the consumer is motivated by a desire for profit, in human services there is no place for the producer's profit-oriented self-interest. *Third*, human services do not produce tangible things for consumption. They serve; they do not make "things" for sale and use. *Fourth*, every human service organization deals with change—change in the individual's life and change in the fabric of community life. The human services organization is alert to the social-political-economic pressures that cause change (and problems) and seeks to give services which will enable people to deal with change and, sometimes, even benefit from change.

Human services is seeking to realign its subsystems into a workable *network* which is most responsive to meeting people's needs to solve their problems. Linking people to services through this network or bridge is the backbone of human services. In addition, several newly-designed human services organizations are developing across the country which embody the profession's goals and philosophy in innovative ways to more fully meet the needs of the whole person. In the future it is anticipated that there will be a growth of these new service models (or modules) which will reinforce the overall network. The three most recent human services organizations are: *The Information and Referral Center;* the *Diagnostic Center;* and the *Multiservice Center.*

The Information and Referral Center is sometimes called the "nucleus" of human services in a community. Usually such a center is a service provided cooperatively by all the subsystems in which they put together a shared fund of information about their respective services and make that knowledge available to anyone who needs it. The Center is usually a small operation, consisting of several people answering telephone inquiries. For example, if a mother needs day care for her children and doesn't know where to go, she can call the Information Center and get a list of day care centers in her area. Information is also provided about any other services available in the community. At the Information Center, there is no counseling or direct service provided. Referral to service is the Center's chief work. Such an Information Center is like a dictionary or a map for people who need to be linked to services. The Information Center can be very helpful to professionals, too. Especially in large urban areas, it isn't always possible for the human services worker to keep up with all the services that exist. She can also call the Information Center when she needs to learn of the existence and location of a specific service. For example, in New York City the Community Council operates an Information Service. Not long ago, a human services worker needed to find Chinese-speaking social services for a gentleman who spoke Cantonese and needed housing and homemaker services. A quick call to the Information Service linked her to an agency in Chinatown to which she could bring the man so that his needs could be met.

The Diagnostic Center is an organization which is more medically oriented, as its name suggests. This Center is manned by professionals who are equipped to conduct diagnostic interviews with people who come to the Center for help in finding resources. In this way, the services of the Center can be more specific and individualized than those of the telephone-based Information Center. However, like the Information Center, the Diagnostic Center does not provide ongoing treatment. Both are intended to make appropriate referrals to human service subsystems where the helping work can take place. Both types of Centers, therefore, should be seen as bridges to service.

The Multiservice Center, unlike the two foregoing organizations, is designed to follow through by providing service in some cases. Sometimes known as a "store front," the Multiservice Center is usually located right in the heart of the community where people can easily walk in and find someone who is able to either help them with problem-solving on the spot or refer them to the appropriate source without undue delay. A Multiservice Center is not intended to be "all things to all people" to the exclusion of the human services subsystems. It is not designed to absorb the others. Rather, it is meant to enhance them. The idea behind the creation of a Multiservice Center is similar to the creation of a supermarket where the consumer can conveniently do "one-stop shopping." For example, there are such centers now operating around the country that bring together as many as twenty-two different human services under one roof! For example, if Mr. Kelly has a variety of needs, he can talk to someone at the Center who can direct him to a law office; a family service agency; and/or a family planning clinic—all located within the Center. Such a Center aims to house and coordinate all the services needed by the people in the community it serves. The Multiservice Center is an exciting answer to the gigantic and impersonalized bureaucracies with which people usually are faced in trying to meet their complex human needs.

These three innovations in programming are concrete evidence of human services philosophy in action. It is predictable that there will be a rapid expansion of such innovative need-meeting services as well as the creation of additional types of responsive programs in the future. However, we cannot assume that such people-centered programs and services will "just happen." They are the product of social policy and planning. Every one of us needs to be alert not only to people's needs, but to the larger influences in our society that will enable human services to develop and sustain programs to meet needs in newer, more comprehensive, and more efficient ways. It is not enough for the human services worker to be skillful in problem-solving with individuals and families. She must also become attuned to identifying problems in the larger society and learning how her profession can have an impact on influencing the development of social policy to solve those larger problems. We mustn't fall into the trap of "not seeing the forest for the trees" because we're so busy with our day-to-day work that we are blissfully ignorant of forces growing in the society to damage the quality of life and interfere with the goals of human services. Nor can we permit ourselves the luxury of assuming that it is not the responsibility of us "little guys" to deal with policy issues.

We should have learned by now in the United States that we cannot always assume that our leaders know what's best or that they will act accordingly, even when they do. In every way we can, each of us has a job to do in furthering the growth of human services policy. Maybe we can't all "march on Washington" every time we want a needed policy developed, but we can write to our legislators and we definitely can vote for people we think have a human services orientation. And, we can and must do our homework. We must continually ask the right questions and try to develop responsive programs so that we are able to *demonstrate* the positive and significant impact of the new network of human services in meeting the needs of the whole person—and thereby in meeting the needs of contemporary society for creating a quality of life which will support satisfying living for all society's people.

BIBLIOGRAPHY

Kahn, Alfred J. *Studies in Social Policy and Planning.* New York: Russell Sage Foundation, 1969.

————. *Theory and Practice of Social Planning.* New York: Russell Sage Foundation, 1969.

Slater, Philip. *The Pursuit of Loneliness: American Culture at the Breaking Point.* Boston: Beacon Press, 1970.

Titmuss, Richard. *Social Policy.* New York: Pantheon Books, 1974.

chapter five

Use of Self

TOOLS OF THE TRADE

Human services workers seem to have been short-changed in a way. Carpenters have their hammers; doctors have medicines. What tools do we in human services have? Ourselves, primarily. To be sure, we have a body of knowledge—which is what this book is all about. But, all the knowledge in the library does not a human services worker make. Rather, our most essential tool is our individual selves. That may sound obvious and even simple. However, when you give some thought to just how complex each of us really is, it becomes clear that using oneself effectively is anything but simple. In order to use oneself to serve another, one must first come to self-understanding.

Why is self-understanding so vitally important? The cornerstone of human services is the relationships we establish with those we are trying to serve. Without a good working relationship as a foundation for your efforts, the services you set out to provide will fall far short of the basic goal of human services—to provide people with services that will support and enhance their lives.

"The road to hell is paved with good intentions." This is particularly true in human services. Good intentions without a solid knowledge base from which to operate and a sound awareness for just who you are and what you're doing in this line of work are not going to be of much long-run help to anyone.

Just what *are* you doing in this line of work anyway? We know you didn't choose human services to get rich or even to be identified with a very prestigious profession. How you answer this question will provide a good entrance into exploring the expectations, values, and needs you bring to your work. Did you choose human services because you enjoy working with people? Because you believe you have some aptitude for working with people? Because you want to be helpful? Because being helpful feels good? These are all perfectly valid reasons for pursuing a career in human services. If, however, your main interest in this field is the hope that you'll be able to find solutions to your own problems in this way, perhaps you should re-examine your motivations. Many people do enter the helping professions for this reason. They are usually sadly disappointed in their work. So are the people they half-heartedly try to serve. One of the fringe benefits of human services is that you will through your experience learn more about yourself and others. But, your role is to do the helping, not to be helped.

Whatever happened to "Lady Bountiful"? The human services are still trying to live down her reputation. Personally, I think she's alive and well and living in a Charles Schultz comic strip, under the assumed name of Lucy. Nowadays, she says things such as, "I love mankind. It's people I can't stand!" Lady Bountiful would surely agree. Whether she's called Lucy or Pollyanna or Goody Two-Shoes, the character is the same: someone who is more interested in the *activities* of helping than in the people needing help. Lady Bountiful would be appalled to learn that we are providing human services because people are entitled to them, not because we're being benevolent towards the "underprivileged."

Assuming that you have thought about your reasons for choosing a career in human services and have decided, with a little healthy selfishness, that this is the career for you, let's now explore how you enter this field. Whether you are employed in a day care center, a nursing home, a school, or a mental institution, you will still be expected to establish a relationship with each person you serve in order to be helpful. Again, *the quality of your relationship is the cornerstone of helping.* Let us first examine what you bring to a professional relationship and then look at the components of an effective relationship between a human services worker and the individual being served.

What one brings to a helping relationship:

Commonality • We are all more alike than different, whether we find ourselves giving help or seeking it. We are all members of a transitional age who share the same planet and the same human needs. In addition to the basic need for food, clothing, and shelter, each of us has equally essential needs for the following.

Belonging • The anthropologists tell us that man is a social animal who thrives and develops through association with his fellow men. All of us identify with a number of social groups which are formal or informal in organization. For example, we interact with our families, with our friends, with fellow students or fellow employees. The sense of belonging we derive from these and the many other groups to which we adhere is essential to our identity and to our well-being. With the sad exception of those few eccentric souls we call hermits or catatonic, people do not prosper in isolation. All of us need to belong, to feel a relatedness to others. While it is true that we also benefit from being alone at times, it is painful to be lonely. People need other people with whom they feel kinship or commonality in order to insure their very survival as human beings. Each of us, at some point, has had the uncomfortable experience of being a complete stranger or total outsider in some social situation. And, each of us can recall the pleasure of seeing familiar faces or of coming home and remember the joy such experiences brought because they carried with them an affirmation of belonging. Especially in today's rapidly changing society where people move around a lot and families are shrinking, those feelings of belonging are becoming rare and precious indeed.

Spheres of Influence • Every individual needs to know not only that he belongs, but that he counts for something with his fellow man. Everyone needs to feel some measure of control over his own life and to achieve some sense of mastery over his environment. Feeling powerless and totally dependent on outside forces robs an individual of his faith in himself and belief in his own worth. (One of the most impressive things about democracy, for example, is that everybody gets a vote and every vote counts. When people don't exercise the right and throw away their votes, they contribute to an undermining of their own power.) It is not necessary to dominate others or to dictate events in order to feel influential. What is important is knowing that your responsible action (or opinion or need) is responded to by others with respect and concern and that you are able, by your own influence and appropriate power, to meet this need for mastery of your own life.

Individuality • While it is essential that we feel secure in belonging, it is equally important that we feel secure in our separateness. Paradoxically, all of us need to know that we are not carbon copies of everyone else in our own or other groups. Clearly, we are all more alike than different, but all of us have at least one special attribute that sets us apart from everybody else. In other words, all of us need to be able to describe ourselves as individuals as well as part of a "we." This ability is, of course, the core of one's identity. Our individuality gives us visibility among our peers. It helps us stand out in a crowd and affirms our selfhood, the source of our personal strength. In our time, it is the people who see themselves as nothing more than nameless faces in a crowd, devoid of uniqueness, who find themselves despairing, invisible. Each of us has a need to strive for individual recognition.

Pleasure • We rarely think of enjoying ourselves as being a basic human need. Yet, enjoyment is truly imperative to living. Pleasure sets living above and apart from merely existing. A sense of humor, a good joke shared or even a silly pun help each of us keep a positive balance in our lives. We all can think of someone we know who seems totally without a sense of humor. Don't we pity him? When we start taking things too seriously, having the ability to laugh at our own mistakes or to see some absurdity around us goes a long way toward helping us readjust our outlook. We probably also know someone who is "all work, no play." These driven people eventually "burn out," never taking time out to please themselves and to enjoy their surroundings to enhance them as human beings. "Having a good time" sounds frivolous, but such good moments are essential to emotional well-being.

Productivity • Being engaged in activity that yields something you have produced is also a basic human need. Idleness spawns depression and a lack of self-esteem. People are producers. They need to do things and to make things. This is not to suggest that every job can offer fulfillment. Nevertheless, each of us has a need to be productive in some meaningful way. The possibilities are endless. Some people feel its a real accomplishment to simonize their cars, or to write poetry, or to make a plant grow, or to play the guitar, or to discover a new star, or even to write a human services textbook. All of these things and countless others are significant in that they provide the doers with a sense of creativity. Each of us needs to know the satisfaction of producing or accomplishing things. We need to feel entitled to pat ourselves on the back for a job well done and we need to be able to point with pride to that job well done.

Direction   •   Each of us has a very basic need to know where we're going. Of course, we aren't born with a blueprint for our lives in hand. As we mature, we draw our own. Many of us don't learn early enough that every step we take determines the next, and we find ourselves going in circles as a result.

Sigmund Freud was once asked to give the criteria of mental health. Instead of responding with a long-winded dissertation on psychological phenomena, he answered simply that an individual's mental health could be measured by one's ability *to love and to work*. It is the people and things we love and the work we do that gives us a sense of direction and guides our lives. People who feel themselves to be directionless, just drifting through life mildly or severely depressed are those who cannot or will not invest themselves in the work they do and cannot or do not love anything or anyone (least of all themselves) with any intensity.

Self-Actualization   •   Each of us has a very basic need to continue developing and growing as an individual. This ongoing process throughout life is called self-actualization. It means that all of us are continually engaged in finding fulfillment to our lives in new and varied ways as we mature. It also means that each of us is engaged in striving to reach the full potential within us. Reaching within ourselves to know and express the many facets of our personalities is truly a lifelong involvement. The goal of "getting it together" is one that can never be completely reached. Nor should it be. Having all the answers can be terribly dull. There's hardly anything more boring (and self-defeating) than complacency. There's an old saying "The more you know, the more you don't know." So it is with each of our lives: there is always more to know, to seek, to experience, to understand, and to enjoy. Those who accept and welcome this outlook are the most thoroughly alive and gratified people among us.

Human Needs

These are the needs which all of us share, whether we find ourselves offering or receiving help. As a human services worker, you bring more than your needs to the helping relationship. You bring who you are. You bring the totality of your own experiences, values, goals, and awareness as well as your personal feelings and aspirations. You bring your own unique history, as it was shaped by the interaction of your growing personality and the world in which you grew up. The values and traditions of society and your particular subculture contribute to the frame of reference from which you view the world. So do the attitudes and biases of your culture. In addition to those things that society tells you are important, you bring those values which you have decided are important to your life. Your background, the accumulation of your life experiences and your feelings all find their way into the helping relationship. The influence they will have in the helping relationship is determined by your awareness of them.

When I was a beginning worker, one of my first assignments was to help an elderly couple who were apparently without interested family and were unable to care for themselves any longer. While visiting them and trying to be helpful, I focused most of my attention and effort on motivating the man in the situation to better organize their daily life. Later, my supervisor asked me who was the "boss" in my own home. I wondered about her question because I was feeling rather proud of myself about helping this couple. I answered that it was my father who made most decisions and was the dominant family member. Knowingly, my supervisor smiled and through a few well-placed questions showed me very effectively how I had mistakenly brought too much of my background to work that day. The couple I was trying to help were both elderly, to be sure. But, the husband was far more senile and less able to meet his own needs than was his wife. Yet, I had plunged ahead, ignoring the woman entirely, because of my assumption that other families functioned just like my own. I learned valuable lessons in helping and in self-awareness that day.

Self-Awareness and Self-Esteem

Self-awareness is our greatest asset and its absence our greatest liability. I can't improve on the Greek counsel, "Know thyself." Only Shakespeare's Polonius did when he said, "To thine own self be true and it will follow, as night the day, thou cans't not be false to any other man." Self-awareness means knowing, in essence, "what makes you tick." It is a knowledge of your own feelings and wants, your attitudes and values, your wishes and fears, your strengths and weaknesses. No one else in this world, not even those closest to you, can ever know you as well as you can know yourself. While we must agree that, "No man is an island" because we are all in numerous ways interdependent, it is also paradoxically true that each of us is an island unto ourselves. As human beings, we can never know total unity with one another. We are islands who are born alone and who must die alone. Certainly, we need and value a sense of belonging and relatedness, but we all strive simultaneously to maintain our individual integrity, to avoid total absorption by and in others. It is a delicate balance to achieve closeness in relationships without losing our selfhood, but a balance that must be maintained. Our awareness of who we are is essential before we can help others.

Self-esteem is closely related to self-awareness. Self-esteem is the conviction you have in your own worth and competence. Self-esteem is born of self-awareness. It is the value you place on yourself, knowing your own assets and liabilities. Having adequate self-esteem means you see yourself clearly—without a smoke-screen of either grandiose fantasies or overgrown humility—and you basically like what you see. That is, though you are well aware that you aren't perfect, you can make peace with your faults and say, with conviction, "Yes, I am o.k." Self-awareness gives one an accurate assessment of personal characteristics. Self-esteem gives one a high positive regard for those characteristics which comprise one's self.

Esteem for others is essential to and derived from self-esteem. Once we can say, "I'm OK," we can also say, "You're OK." Unfortunately, it is quite true that many individuals who are certain of the worth of others, have enormous difficulty convincing themselves that they, too, are worthwhile. There are also some who sing their own praises at a moment's notice, but never have a nice word to say about anyone else. In neither example are the people described blessed with true self-esteem.

Esteem is channeled in two directions: inward and outward, towards oneself and towards others. Healthy self-esteem will generate esteem of others and the knowledge that you are esteemed by others will enhance your own self-esteem. It is undeniably true that others' opinions about us have a strong effect on our self-feelings, positively or negatively. Nevertheless, a person with healthy self-esteem does his own evaluation of his worth and competence. He does not allow others to define or evaluate him. Many people are guided in their self-evaluating and in their general living by the question, "What will people think . . . ?" These people allow their self-esteem to be determined totally by others instead of allowing their own self-awareness to assure them of their worthiness.

Self-esteem makes us more alive, more open to life, and gives us more freedom and more control and infinitely more ability to realize more of our potential for an enriched and gratifying life. Self-esteem gives us strength within ourselves which we can readily tap in our work with others. You will readily see the calming effect of such strength on the people you'd like to help. Holding oneself in esteem says to those who come to you for help, "I like myself. I am competent. I believe that both you and I are worthwhile. I want to be of help." There is an abundance of emotional energy required of the helping person. Without unshakable self-esteem, your energy will soon be depleted in trying to make yourself feel good. That energy should be free to utilize in helping someone else and it only can be if your self-esteem is secure. Oh, yes, we all have days when we don't like what we see in the mirror and we aren't too pleased with ourselves. On days like that, a person with self-esteem can take a sympathetically long look at what's making him feel uncomfortable with himself and go about doing whatever it takes to feel better. All of us need a little pampering with more than a little regularity. The person with adequate self-esteem accepts this need. Self-esteem does not mean blind devotion to oneself. It does mean acceptance of yourself on the days you make mistakes as well as on the days you feel on top of the world.

COMPONENTS OF A HELPING RELATIONSHIP

So, you see, you bring many things to a helping relationship before you even say hello. In addition to all that's been discussed, you bring your professional knowledge and skill and your conscious awareness that you are setting out to develop a professional relationship with someone you want to help. Because you are not in the business of making friends of your clients or establishing casual acquaintanceships with them, you know that you must work very hard at keeping your own needs out of the relationship.

The two of you have come together to focus on the other person's needs, not yours. This is the key to professional behavior: knowledge that your client is not there to fulfill your needs. It is a difficult task to use one's self to help. What you choose to reveal about yourself can either help or hinder. A good yardstick for deciding how much to reveal about yourself is to decide how helpful such a revelation might be. For example, when someone tells you about an incident that has made them sad and depressed, it could be helpful to say, "I know how you feel. I've felt that way, too." It would be very unhelpful to go on to reveal depressing experiences of your own. Others are rarely as interested in us as we are, particularly when they're hurting. How you use yourself and what you reveal about yourself should always be guided by the helpfulness that will result.

In a helping relationship, there are a number of qualities the helper must display. These qualities are demonstrated through a professional use of self. These qualities are the essential components of a helping relationship:

Genuineness • The helping person must be perceived as a "real" person with spontaneity and capacity for responsiveness. A genuine person is not role-playing or maintaining a facade or "playing it cool," but is reacting honestly to life and to others.

Acceptance • The helping person is convinced of the other person's worth as an individual and conveys respect and caring for him. She is also flexible, able to attune herself to the other person's tempo, rather than insisting on her own timetable.

Empathy • The helping person conveys sensitivity to the other and tries to understand what walking in the other guy's shoes may feel like. Although she may never have shared the situations and experiences of the other person, she can understand the feelings that result. She tries to "tune in" so that she will hear the other person's music as well as his words.

Invite Trust • Through acceptance and respect, the helping person invites the other person to trust in her objectivity and feel secure that she is respected and cared for as a worthwhile individual. Together, through trust, they develop a relationship in which the person seeking help can confidently reveal his feelings and his needs.

Clarity • The helping person is aware that her words and actions and even her body language are received as messages by the person seeking her help. The messages must be clear and congruent, free of any "do as I say, not as I do" implications.

If you are genuine, warm, accepting, empathetic, trustworthy, and clear, will you be helpful? Not always. Sometimes you will fail—either because you didn't convey these qualities sufficiently or because the person you thought you were helping simply wasn't ready for your help. However, if you actively engage yourself in incorporating these components in your relationships with your clients, you will be of help, of great help most of the time.

Providing human services requires knowing oneself and applying that knowledge to the development of helping relationships. It is necessary and essential to know oneself before one can know another or be helpful to him. Knowing oneself takes time and can never be complete. You are, after all, a complicated human being and an ever-changing and growing one. How do you begin? There are a number of questions developed by Naomi Brill[1] which serve as useful guides for self-exploration:

- **How do I think and feel about myself?**
- **How do I deal with my own fundamental needs?**
- **What is my value system, and how does it define my behavior and my relationships with other people?**
- **How do I relate to the society in which I live and work?**
- **What is my life style?**
- **What is my basic philosophy?**

Another route for exploration is to look closely at your own assets and liabilities, your strengths and weaknesses. What are your strong points? Your weak ones? What about yourself are you proudest of? What would you like to change? Do you feel that the person you present to the world is the "real" you or are you different from the way you act? How do you find gratification? What are your inner resources? What do you enjoy? What do you strive for?

The answers to such questions require a good deal of thought and reflection. Take your time in finding them.

Another good clue to self-understanding is an awareness of how

---

[1]Naomi Brill, *Working with People*, p. 4.

you use time. Do you "kill" it? Do you have enough of it? How do you spend it? In *Born to Win,*[2] James and Jongeward have updated Ecclessiastics in this lovely poem, reminding us that

> For everything there is a season and for every activity a time.
> A time to be aggressive and a time to be passive,
> A time to be together and a time to be alone,
> A time to fight and a time to love,
> A time to work and a time to play,
> A time to cry and a time to laugh,
> A time to confront and a time to withdraw,
> A time to speak and a time to be silent,
> A time to hurry and a time to wait.

How you use time is certainly significant to who you are.

We can look further into ourselves by following Freud's dictum, "to love and to work." Try to understand who you love and why. Know what is most important to you and why. Add to this an understanding of why you do the work you do and what importance it holds for you, and you will have a good deal of vital information for increased self-awareness.

There is yet another way to begin to know yourself better and deeper. Try to define a "winner" and a "loser." What makes a winning personality and what makes a losing one? Which one do you have? How do you know?

Summary

These then are some techniques for developing the fundamentals of self-awareness. Each of us in the helping professions must take on a commitment to engage ourselves in learning who we are and in coming to terms with that knowledge. There is yet another commitment we make regarding ourselves—a commitment to our own growth as individuals and as professionals. Each of us must continually strive to grow in self-understanding and in consequent increased professional competence. To accomplish this, we begin with the belief that everyone is capable of growth and change, of becoming more of a person than they already are. This faith in people and their capacities is the heart of human services.

---

[2]Muriel James and Dorothy Jongeward, *Born to Win,* p. 4.

Choosing a career in human services carries with it an awesome responsibility to know yourself and others as fully as possible. A human services worker should have a clear perception of life and of herself. She should be able to discern what is real from her fantasies. She should be involved in living, committed to life and open to its experiences. She shouldn't get her facts and her fears mixed up. A human services worker has developed a sense of direction by which she is able to offer help. She understands people's interdependence with one another and seeks to utilize her knowledge of herself and of society in the service of others. She has what Albert Schweitzer called a *reverence for life*—an intrinsic faith and respect for every living thing, including herself.

Using yourself through knowing yourself is the essential tool of the human services. To the Greek adage, "Know thyself," I would only add, "And, trust thyself." When you come to know and accept yourself, you will indeed be well able to trust yourself as a person and professional.

BIBLIOGRAPHY

Berne, Eric. *What Do You Say After You Say Hello?* New York: Grove Press, 1972.

Branden, Nathaniel. *The Psychology of Self-Esteem.* Los Angeles: Nash, 1969.

Brill, Naomi. *Working with People: The Helping Process.* New York: Lippincott, 1973.

Fromm, Erich. *The Art of Loving.* New York: Harper and Row, 1956.

Harris, Thomas. *I'm OK—You're OK.* New York: Harper and Row, 1967.

James, Muriel, and Jongeward, Dorothy. *Born to Win.* Reading, Mass.: Addison-Wesley Publishing, 1971.

Kiernan, Thomas. *A Treasury of Albert Schweitzer.* New York: Citadel Press, 1965.

Maslow, Abraham. *The Farther Reaches of Human Nature.* New York: Viking Press, 1971.

May, Rollo. *Man's Search for Himself.* New York: W.W. Norton, 1953.

Rogers, Carl. *On Becoming A Person.* Boston: Houghton Mifflin, 1961.

Stringer, Lorene. *The Sense of Self: A Guide to How We Mature.* Philadelphia: Temple University Press, 1971.

chapter six

Understanding People

People can be magnificent and they can be mystifying. It all depends on how well you understand them. The first step towards a workable understanding of others is a solid base of self-awareness and acceptance, as discussed in the preceeding chapter. A significant aspect of self-understanding is the knowledge that we are all alike in many respects and share the same fundamental needs. Some of those needs arise from our biological requirements; others from our culture; and still others from our psychological make-up. People and their needs are always *multidimensional;* a complex panorama of attitudes, inclinations, and actions.

No one else can ever know us as well or completely as we can know ourselves. We can know many things about others, but never all there is to know. People don't fit under any kind of microscope. In attempting to understand people it is very true that "a little bit of knowledge is a dangerous thing." All of us have had the experience of relying on our first impressions of people and later finding ourselves very wrong about those impressions and those people. In all social interactions, and particularly in helping situations, it's probably safe to assume that first impressions are generally wrong, or at least inadequate. People are rarely what they seem at first glance. People are far too complicated to be sized up in one brief encounter. That's what makes folks so fascinating.

BASE OF UNDERSTANDING

The best approach for the human services worker who would understand people is to take a patient and objective *wait-and-see attitude* towards others. Every individual is the totality of his or her life experiences, innate capacities, needs, values, goals, aptitudes, at-

103

titudes, and opportunities. Each life has a unique pattern created by the social, genetic, biochemical, and characterological forces that all of us possess in combinations that are never quite the same in any other individual. As if the complexity of the factors described above aren't enough to show us how complicated people are, it must also be remembered that those factors are constantly interacting and often changing. People are *dynamic*. No one is a "finished product." The impact of relationships with other people and with the environment will certainly make it impossible for anyone to remain completely the same from day to day or year to year. I'm certainly not the same person I was five years ago. My life experiences since then have continued to shape me and will continue to do so to some extent for the rest of my life. This is true for all of us.

If people and things are constantly changing, how can a human services worker possibly learn enough about the people she wants to help? It isn't easy! Learning to know another person is an ongoing process, just as time-consuming as learning to know yourself. However, it is not necessary for a worker to thoroughly "psychoanalyze" every person she wants to help. Instead, she should begin with a basic understanding of the forces (and the interplay between those forces) that effect all human beings. Obviously, the human services worker who chooses a career in the mental health field will concentrate on increasing her knowledge of psychodynamics; while the health field will require more emphasis on body chemistry and functions; and community work will require focus on the effect of environmental forces on people's lives. Clearly, this text cannot meet the needs of all those varying points of emphasis. That specialized knowledge related to the theory of a particular human services subsystem must be found from other sources. Nevertheless, every human services worker should enter the field with a beginning understanding that people are shaped and molded throughout their lives by their bodies, their minds, their emotions, and by the world around them.

For discussion purposes, considerations of biology, culture, and psychology have been separated from each other in this chapter. It cannot be overemphasized, however, that such separations are definitely artificial. The core philosophy of human services stands staunchly against compartmentalizing people according to their various attributes. If one is to begin to understand people, one must not lose sight of the fact that people are multidimensional. The making of a person is like baking a cake. Once you've mixed the ingredients, you

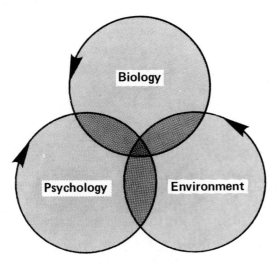

INTERACTING PERSONALITY FORCES

can't take them back out again. You just have to remember that there are lots of ingredients.

Undoubtedly, every student entering human services has already been exposed to many theories about culture, personality, and biology. During your professional life, you will also surely be confronted with many more, sometimes conflicting theories. Human services is essentially pragmatic. It attempts to utilize whatever works in helping instead of being bound to one school of thought or body of theories. It is *eclectic*. It uses knowledge from many sources and integrates them in the most helpful way.

For example, there are several theories in the psychiatric literature about what motivates people and what methods help people change. Those theories are sometimes diametrically opposed. Many professionals profess an allegiance to only one theory and forget the rest. That's rather wasteful of human resources! It would be much more useful to the people asking for help if all of us professionals could keep an open mind to each theory and use as much of it as may be helpful. In my social work practice, I've come to call this a "bits-and-pieces approach" to helping. I've tried to incorporate many theories into my work without buying any one of them in its entirety. I have learned a great deal about people and, consequently, have been increasingly helpful to them by borrowing a little bit from psychoanalytic thinkers; a little from behavior modification advocates;

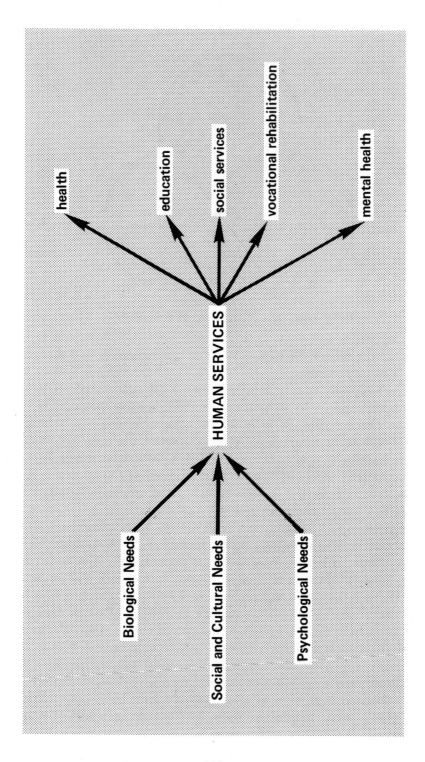

a little more from Transactional Analysis; and so on. The important thing is to maintain a professional commitment to keeping aware of new ideas and concepts and then using them meaningfully to be helpful. There is nothing holy about sticking exclusively to one school of thought (as if it were a fraternity or something). Human services has moved beyond those traditional, self-limiting boundaries.

BIOLOGICAL CONSIDERATIONS

One of the oldest semi-scientific debates with which great minds have struggled is the "nature vs. nurture" dilemma. Is man's development shaped more by nature (genetic inheritance) or by the treatment (nurture or lack of it) he receives after entering this world? Needless to say, the debates continue. There doesn't seem to be a clear-cut answer. As a matter of fact, scientific developments and discoveries in recent years have tended to blur the issues even further. It's probably just as well to let the matter rest with agreement that nature and nurture *together* are pivotal to shaping people's lives.

A person's constitutional endowment—his biological heritage— is clearly influential in determining the course his life will take. There are three aspects of a person's biology which must be considered in any attempt to understand the total person. Those aspects are:

- **Physical self—health, physique**
- **Temperment**
- **Intelligence**

Physical Self

The size, shape and relative healthy or unhealthy functioning of a person's body will have a lot to do with his ability to deal with other people, the outside world, and even himself. The world is perceived very differently by a handicapped person who has been denied the asset of a fully functioning body. This is, of course, also true for a person plagued by pain and physical discomfort. Just recall how bleak things tend to look to you when you're wrestling with a bout of the flu and you can imagine how others who are either acutely or chronically ill must feel.

Physical appearance also has an impact on every person. Here we are not talking about the kind of clothes a person wears or whether he is neatly dressed. Rather, we're considering what he looks like— short, fat, handsome, bald, muscular, scarred, or whatever. A person's own reaction to his body compounded by the reactions of others has a decided influence on that person. In thinking about physical appearance, it is already apparent that other forces enter into what a person looks like: e.g., a fat lady could go on a diet; a badly scarred man could have plastic surgery. The person's self-esteem and cultural expectations about physical appearance have a lot to do with physical appearance, to be sure.

Temperment

Temperment is now increasingly being considered part of a person's biological make-up. Earlier, it was believed that an individual's essential tempermant (whether gregarious; quiet; argumentative; passive; etc.) was the end result of his upbringing. This coincided with the belief that a newborn was totally without any other attributes besides his physical self as he emerged into the world. He was believed to be *tabula rasa,* an empty page on which life experiences would write a story and form a temperment. Today, however, we are realizing that even newborn infants have distinct personalities. Certainly no one is suggesting that those personalities are fully formed so early in life. But, it does appear that every baby comes equipped with his own unique temperment.

We are learning a great deal about people through the application of scientific methods, it is true. Just the same, there are some areas—and temperment is one of them—where the nature of people is still puzzling. We don't know why some people are more able to cope than others with similar life experiences. Nor do we comprehend why one person may be overcome by far less stress than another. There is an illuminating anecdote about the mysteries of individual temperment that goes something like this.

One Christmas morning a pair of little twin brothers came to see what Santa had left under the tree for them. What they found was a huge sack of horse manure. The first brother was terribly upset, wept bitter tears, and was convinced that his gift meant that he was worthless and unloved. The second brother reacted very differently and jumped for joy. When the unhappy twin asked how he could possibly be so delighted with their present, the answer was, "With all that manure, there's got to be a pony around here somewhere!"

By temperment, one boy was an optimist and his brother, a pessimist. How did that happen when all other things in their genes and home lives were equal? We simply don't know. We only know that each person is unique from birth on.

Intelligence

Intelligence is a biological consideration which receives a lot of attention in our achievement-oriented society. It is clear that society values high intelligence, but it is not always clear that nature and nurture are doing their best to provide a person with the opportunity to make maximal use of his native intelligence.

Attempting a thorough definition of the term intelligence deserves a whole book in itself. We all know of people who might rank in the genius range in an I.Q. test, but who barely have an ounce of common sense. Intelligence is the sum total of one's mental faculties and, as far as I know, we haven't come up with an adequate way to tap and score them all yet. While I.Q. tests certainly have some value, there is no reason to believe that the tests have been perfected enough to present a complete picture of any individual's full range of intellectual abilities. Still, they can be of some usefulness and every human services worker should be at least acquainted with them. The most widely used intelligence tests are: Weschsler Adult Intelligence Test (WAIS); Weschsler Intelligence Scale for Children (WISC); Bender/Gestalt; and Stanford/Binet. The notion that a person has a "fixed intelligence" is not highly regarded today. I.Q. test scores can vary substantially for the same individual at different points in his life, depending on the interaction of the many forces involved in his life.

In the United States, the "average" person's intelligence is expected to be reflected in an I.Q. (Intelligence Quotient) score of 100–110. A person who scores far above, up to the top score in the test range, is considered superior or genius. The person whose score falls a certain amount below the average is considered to be mentally retarded. *Mental Retardation* means that an individual's intellectual capacities are impaired. There are several degrees of retardation:

I.Q.	83–68	Borderline intelligence
	67–52	Mild retardation
	51–36	Moderate retardation

| 35–21 | Severe retardation |
| 20– 0 | Profound retardation |

Interest and significant research in mental retardation have only been undertaken wholeheartedly in the United States in the last few decades. Previously, the person with impaired intelligence was called an "idiot" or "imbecile" and virtually ignored by his society who didn't consider him much of a human being. Now, as we emerge from those dark times, we realize that individuals with I.Q.'s even in the profoundly retarded range do have rights and some abilities which they are entitled to develop as fully as possible.

These three biological considerations—physical self, temperment, and intelligence—are significant factors in enabling a person to deal effectively with his world. Any student of human services who wishes to understand people can begin by assessing them in terms of their biological endowments.

CULTURAL CONSIDERATIONS

To understand people more fully, the student needs next to combine her knowledge of biological influences with some knowledge of the impact of cultural forces on people. Nobody lives in a vacuum. Nobody becomes a person without other people. We are all significantly influenced by the array of cultural traditions, roles, and expectations that surround us and everybody else.

Have you ever heard of Wolf Boy? Some years ago, a missionary couple in India was killed and their infant son was taken in by a mother wolf who raised him with her own cubs. Eventually, the boy was found and taken to England where it was hoped that he could be helped to become a person. Wolf Boy was, however, not a person. He was, in fact if not in body, a wolf. He ate only raw meat, ran on all fours, snarled at humans, and behaved in all other ways like the wolf he was raised to be. Wolf Boy died recently, never having been a person. His true story dramatically demonstrates the vast importance of culture on people.

If any one of us had been left to our own devices in our infant cribs, we'd probably still be lying there. We needed adults to encourage and direct our development. This process is called *socialization*. Children, through their participation in the socialization process in

which they engage with others (parents, adults, and other children)
learn the basic "rules of the game" for living and behaving appropriately within their culture. In almost every culture, socialization
begins within the context of the family. Parents, siblings, and other
relatives teach the child right from wrong regarding almost every
imaginable social interaction and situation. The "do's" and "don'ts"
include language, dress, manners, habits, sleep patterns, as well as
more abstract beliefs and values, such as religious convictions, patrio-
tism, superstitions, and such. In modern industrialized societies, socialization responsibilities are now shared by the family with the
school, the church, the neighborhood, and even the television set.
Together, these social systems contribute to the child's socialization
and to his cultural conditioning.

   Cultural conditioning, unlike socialization, doesn't end with
childhood. People continue to be influenced (or conditioned) by their
culture throughout their lives. The field of sociology provides us with
an impressive list of factors that go into cultural conditioning. They
include:

role expectations	values
traditions	role models
reference groups	status
class	mobility
deviance	norms
taboos	

Although we may not be familiar with these terms, each of us has and
continues to be influenced and directed by them. Our culture has
welcomed us with the proviso that we must meet its expectations and
observe its restrictions. A firm knowledge of these sociological terms
and their implicit cultural considerations is enormously significant to
broadening our fundamental understanding of people.

   Our culture has been here long before we were. Over time, it
has developed a set of social values and traditions as well as outlines
for appropriate behavior (called *norms*) to which society's members
are taught and expected to adhere. The culture has also divided itself
into *classes* (upper, middle, and lower) and has assigned status to
people and classes according to its priorities and values. As noted
earlier, our society places great value on performance, achievement,
and intelligence. Therefore, the society will also give highest status
and class assignments to people who are most intelligent and good

achievers. Furthermore, society has already charted out the means by which people can change their status and/or class and their access to social mobility—movement between statuses and/or classes. Again, in our particular society, achievement is most likely to assure movement up the social ladder.

People move about in society playing assorted *social roles*. All of us have many roles to play. When sociologists use the term "role" it does not imply make-believe or play-acting. Rather, "social role" refers to the duties and responsibilities of an individual that must be undertaken in conjunction with a specific social assignment. For example, being a mother is a social role. So is being a student; a teacher; a clerk; an adolescent; and so on. People are expected to perform in many social roles every day—and in some of them simultaneously. Today, for example, my social roles so far have been: teacher; counselor; friend; daughter; housekeeper; and writer. And the day isn't over yet!

Every social role carries with it certain expectations, both for the society and for the person in the role itself. For instance, society expects a mother to teach, nurture and protect her children so that they can grow up to be healthy and well-functioning. A mother may expect that if she does her job well and makes her children happy and healthy, she will receive recognition and affection from her family (and possibly from others) for a job well done. If you want to understand a person, taking inventory of the social roles he is required to play as well as the roles he desires to fulfill will help you immeasurably.

Reference groups and role models are the culture's agents for assigning "job descriptions" about role expectations. Most of us started out with families. They were our first *reference group*—our mirror of cultural norms and expectations. People use their reference group as a yardstick to measure their own behavior or accomplishments. If your reference group is the people in your neighborhood, the estimation you place on yourself and on your achievements will reflect very closely how you believe you measure up to their expectations and qualifications. Not everybody keeps the same reference group throughout his life. There are some of us for whom our family's opinions, values, and approval will always have highest priority in our life decisions. But, for others, this doesn't remain so after childhood. For them, the significant reference group may become the bowling team, the college faculty, the church group, the block association or any other group with whom they closely identify. Then there are some people who may touch base with several reference groups, but who are basically influenced by their own values and opinions. Such people become, in effect, their own reference groups—at least in part. Such people are called *inner-directed.* Their opposites are called *other-directed* because they are very much influenced by what others think of them and expect of them.

All of us, when we were growing up, had many *role models.* These were people we chose to imitate and pattern our behavior after. Our earliest role models were probably our parents. Later, a favorite teacher, movie star, or sports figure would serve as the "model." People tend to give up their hero-worship tendencies as they get older. Nevertheless, all of us have certain people in our immediate lives, or more famous people, whom we admire greatly. Understanding both the reference groups and role models by which a person is influenced are two additional cultural factors with great bearing on that person, and about which a helping person should have some knowledge.

Culture is of great significance to people, as we have already seen, because it provides them with information and training about how to behave in the world. Culture is a powerful shaper of people's lives for another reason, too. To a great extent, it is culture that provides (or withholds) from people the opportunities they need for living gratifying lives. As discussed more fully in the chapter on Social Policy, it is cultural values which determine how a society's resources are to be distributed and, therefore, which members—all, some, or few—are entitled to have as much as they need of society's resources in order to live. In the United States, we are fond of saying that there is "equal opportunity" for everyone to make use of society's resources according to their individual abilities and needs. That statement is somewhat misleading. People's opportunities vary according to their status, their class, their roles, and even their biology. Healthy people with highest roles, status, and class will have the best opportunity for using and the most access to society's resources.

An attempt to understand people by learning about their cultural backgrounds must include not only consideration of their positions in society (roles, status, class), but also an awareness of the opportunities available to them in society according to those positions. Culture shapes people in many ways. The combination of "nature and nurture" is always a significant determinant of people's lives and the view they take of their lives.

PSYCHOLOGICAL CONSIDERATIONS

"Nature and nurture" make a unique person. There now exists an enormous body of knowledge about individual psychology which enables us to look more closely at various aspects of personality and to understand ourselves and others better. But, we still don't know the whole story.

It is probably a very human tendency to be uncomfortable with "loose ends." People like certainty; they like to know the "whole" story. That's one reason why we've developed *labels*. We may label a person smart, dumb, "crazy," "normal," nice, and thousands of other things. By labelling a person there's a sense of having some certainty about who that person is and of having some ability to predict his behavior. In human services, however, we know that people are always bigger and better than their labels. The *whole person* defies such "pigeonholing." Furthermore, the labels we use are far from precise. Labels, in truth, are never as definite as $1 + 1 = 2$.

As you begin to work in human services, it will help you immensely to understand people, if you also understand that people really are bigger than their labels: things are rarely black or white; they're usually various shades of gray. Any psychologist worth his salt can find something wrong with anybody and pin some label on each of us. I don't know anyone without at least one "hang-up." Do you? What is "normal"? What is "crazy"? And, how do you classify all the behavior in between? Every individual has a unique combination of strengths and weaknesses which are his equipment for dealing with the world. The "normal" person simply has better internal equipment for dealing with life than does the "crazy" person. There are very few of us running around thinking we are Napoleon. And, there are even fewer of us who have it "all together" in every aspect of our lives. The overwhelming majority of us have psychological equipment which puts us somewhere in the middle of the continuum from "normal" to "crazy." What is this equipment?

Attributes of the "Ideal Person"

The preceding chapter on Use of Self has already outlined many of the attributes of good psychological equipment. Generally, a person with optimal equipment has good skills at interpersonal relationships and at problem-solving based on sound judgment about himself and clear perception of the world outside him. Such an *Ideal Person* would have all of the following attributes:

- flexibility and adaptability in dealing with changes and stress
- good ability to tolerate frustration and to handle failure
- stable values and ideals
- a sense of personal and social responsibility
- a healthy self-interest
- competence in relationships and at tasks
- productivity
- vitality and enthusiasm
- staying power and concentration
- good judgment and reality-testing
- a capacity to plan for the future
- a range of interests and commitments
- authenticity
- self-sufficiency

Needless to say, the "Ideal Person" does not exist. People simply aren't made that way. Nature and nurture do not create perfect specimens.

Some Psychological Terms

The "Ideal Person" we've been discussing would be called an individual who is "normal," with good "mental health." The following review of psychological terms for mental states and disorders is an

attempt to familiarize the human services student with the most frequently used diagnostic labels given to people.

Normal • A person is considered normal when he or she is
able to function effectively in order to meet society's expectations, and to meet his own needs for a satisfying life.
The normal person has, as Freud put it, the greatest
ability "to love and to work."

Neurotic • A person is considered neurotic when he is involved in conflicts within himself that prevent him from
functioning effectively, enjoying life, and realizing his full
potential. Neurotics develop symptoms which further
interfere with their ability to function and to have peace of
mind. The most common neurotic symptoms are:

anxiety reactions • the person is virtually immobilized
by vague feelings of fear and dread, sometimes sharpening
to panic (for no real reason) or dulled by chronic fatigue,
depression, and listlessness.

phobias • the person has an intense and unrealistic fear
of certain objects or situations. A high degree of anxiety is
present and the person generally avoids the feared thing.
Some common phobias are:

agoraphobia—fear of open places
claustrophobia—fear of closed places
acrophobia—fear of heights
zoophobia—fear of animals (or, perhaps just one specific animal)

hysterical behaviors • the person converts his fears into
bodily symptoms or personality changes. Hysterical symptoms include:
conversion reactions—in which the individual may experience paralysis, blindness, or deafness for no
organic reason
amnesia—in which an individual forgets his own identity
dissociative states—in which the person may have several "split" personalities

hypochondriac • the person demonstrates habitual over-concern with health and has unrealistic convictions or fears about being ill.

depressive reactions • the person is so unhappy (about nothing in particular) that everything looks so bleak he takes an "I don't care" attitude and is unable to be optimistic about anything

obsessive/compulsive reactions • the person becomes overly preoccupied either with a particular idea or object or with some sort of ritualistic, repetitive behavior.

Sociopathic • A person is called a sociopath (or designated as having a *character disorder*) when he does not conform to society's expectations and is, on the contrary, motivated only to gratify himself. Pathological liars and criminals as well as people who seem to be without conscience are referred to as sociopaths.

Psychotic • A person is called psychotic when it is evident that his grasp on reality is very distorted and he is unable to distinguish between facts, fears, and fantasies to such an extent that he cannot function effectively to meet his own needs or fulfill societal roles.

The two major categories of psychosis are:

Schizophrenia • the person's thinking (at least in some aspects) is illogical, magical, and fragmented to such a severe extent that his self-understanding and his perceptions of the world outside him are markedly unrealistic. The most well-known (though not the most common) schizophrenic reaction is *paranoia*, in which the individual is convinced that "people are out to get him" either by physically hurting him or doing him other injustice. The paranoiac is the epitome of suspiciousness and mistrust in others or the world in general.

Manic-Depressive Reaction • the individual experiences profound mood-swings from euphoria to despondency, with intensity beyond normal experiences. The swings continue in recurring cycles, much like the movements of a pendulum.

Transactional Analysis

A relatively new school of psychological theory known as Transactional Analysis has much to offer the layman, student, and professional in the way of new insights and terminology as well as concepts about personality. In his well-known book *I'm OK—You're OK,* Dr. Thomas Harris explains that there are four possible life positions people may take in relation to themselves and others. These are:

I'm not OK—You're OK • The person who takes this position believes himself to be a helpless and rather worthless child and spends his time seeking the approval and affection of others in order to try to bolster his self-esteem.

I'm not OK—You're not OK • The person who takes this position believes not only in his own worthlessness, but also that other people are not worth much either. He generally feels that people are hurtful and not trustworthy and prefers to withdraw from them.

I'm OK—You're not OK • The person who takes this position has overcome feelings of worthlessness in himself, but remains sure that others are not worthy of his affection and that he, therefore, has no responsibility to anyone besides himself.

I'm OK—You're OK • The person who takes this position values himself and he values others. He has solid self-esteem and enjoys good relationships with other people.

It is not difficult to see that the traditional labels could readily fit into the four life positions outlined by Harris. Together, these theoretical perspectives can double the student's reference base for understanding people. To these, a third theoretical framework needs to be added which is also extremely useful. This is the concept of "Eight Stages of Man" developed by Erik Erikson in his monumental work, *Childhood and Society.*

"Eight Stages of Man"

According to Dr. Erikson, the human personality develops from infancy to maturity by passing through eight maturational steps. At each step along the way, there are certain developmental tasks required of the individual which must be mastered before he can continue with his development. These steps, briefly, are:

1. ● *Basic Trust*   As early as infancy, a person is confronted with his first developmental task: the establishment of trust in others and in the outside world. The person who has had the benefit of caring, consistent mothering will be able to trust. When this has not been his experience, deep mistrust will be his fundamental orientation to life.

2. ● *Autonomy*   As a toddler, an individual must learn to "stand on his own two feet" both literally and figuratively. He must begin to feel some satisfaction in his own abilities as well as faith in his capacities to fulfill others' expectations. If, however, the individual is confronted with overwhelming expectations and insufficient opportunities to master his tasks, he will be filled with feelings of doubt, shame, or inferiority instead of security.

3. ● *Initiative*   As the child gets older, a satisfactory combination of nature and nurture should encourage him to take the initiative to satisfy his curiosity and learn new things. Without a supportive environment, however, he is more likely to learn to feel intense guilt about what he cannot accomplish instead of feeling secure enough to take increasing initiative.

4. ● *Industry*   The school-aged child learns that he can win recognition by learning and producing. If he is able to master the tasks of the schoolroom, he will increase his sense of personal competence. If he cannot, he will instead despair.

5. ● *Identity*   At adolescence, the maturing person must master the tasks involved in answering the pivotal ques-

tion, "Who am I?" During the teen years, people stabilize their feelings about themselves and their world into a meaningful whole so that they are able to recognize and stand up for who they are and also set life goals based on that understanding. The individual who has not been able to consolidate his personality during adolescence is left with confusion rather than understanding about his identity and his goals.

6 • *Intimacy* In young adulthood, the person with a stable identity is now confronted with the task of establishing and maintaining satisfying involvements with others. The person who is not secure in his own identity cannot fulfill this task adequately and is left with a sense of isolation from others rather than an ability to achieve closeness with them and hold some commitment to them.

7 • *Generactivity* In adulthood, the person's task centers on bringing forth and instructing the next generation. Parenthood is obviously the most likely means of accomplishing this task, but adults who are not parents are also expected to have some interests which go beyond themselves. Even if those interests are unrelated to child-rearing, it is important for the adult to be able to invest himself in some larger concerns. Without them, his task unaccomplished, he is likely to feel personally impoverished and stagnant.

8 • *Ego Integrity* The aging person is confronted with the task of deciding whether he and his life had meaning and dignity. If he believes this is so, he will be heir to a sense of emotional integration and a feeling of oneness with the human community. If, however, the person feels bitter or unfulfilled, he can only face his remaining years and his ultimate death with despair.

As implied in the Eriksonian framework (and more fully in his writings), people are confronted throughout their lives with a series of tasks that can "make or break them," so to speak. Erikson also believes that people can return to uncompleted tasks later in life and fulfill them then. For example, even a person whose experiences as an infant were so negative as to leave him with deep distrust of others (e.g., "I'm OK–You're not OK) can, through later experiences, learn to trust. Similarly, a person who was a failure in school can later learn to master the tasks needed for achieving a sense of industry which he wasn't able to do then. The message is clear: People can and do change and grow throughout their lives. It simply isn't true to say, "once a neurotic always a neurotic" or to feel, "I will everlastingly be not OK." Because people are dynamic and have within them a powerful drive towards inner stability and positive growth, they can and do change in ways to improve their capacities for plain, old-fashioned happiness. It happens every day.

PEOPLE WITH PROBLEMS

People have problems when their needs are not being met. We know that all people have needs related to:

- **life supports (food, clothing, shelter)**
- **pleasure**
- **productivity**
- **belonging**
- **recognition and esteem**
- **meaningful relationships**
- **durable values**
- **a sense of direction**
- **individuality**
- **mastery and competence**
- **an opportunity for personal growth**

Everybody has problems. Most of them are caused by some sort of conflict between people's personal needs and the larger society's priorities. The problems are often compounded because something in the individual's make-up—either his biological self, his cultural background, or his psychological orientation—isn't working well for him. When external demands, choices, expectations, or changes occur which are inconsistent with a person's internal needs, he must rely on his personal resources—his biological, cultural, and psychological gifts—to resolve the conflict for his benefit.

Throughout most of human history, it was generally accepted that when people's needs weren't adequately met it was their own fault and no one else's responsibility. Now, however, we are coming to the humanistic realization that this isn't so. We are all interdependent and, therefore, when someone's needs are not being met, it means that society has a responsibility to find out how to help him solve his problem. That is, after all, what human services is all about! A human services worker always focuses on solving the person's problem, not on blaming him for his inadequacies, conflicts, or lack of opportunities.

The task confronting the human services worker who would be helpful to a person with a problem is to mobilize all the necessary community resources along with her own professional skill to bring the person what he needs and to enable the person to make the most or even enlarge on his own personal equipment for dealing with problems and conflicts. People can change. We know that they are not already locked into one mold by nature and nurture. Society can change, too, in the direction of becoming more responsive to its people and their needs.

UNFINISHED BUSINESS

Obviously, the discussions in this chapter are only the briefest introduction to the fields of knowledge that are adding to our understanding of people. Remember that "a little bit of knowledge is a dangerous thing." Please don't assume that these few pages provide the beginning worker with sufficient background to fully understand people—even the finest scholars of biology, psychology and sociology don't fully understand people. There's too much to know.

Not only are the sciences "unfinished business," so are people! To repeat, people should be considered as "in progress,"—in a continual state of "becoming." Faith in people's continuing growth and ongoing potential are essential for every human services worker. Probably a little harder to come by is an equal amount of faith in society's ability to grow in responsiveness to people. Yet, that kind of faith is needed, too.

The reader may be a little apprehensive by now—wondering just *how much* she will have to learn about the biology, sociology, and psychology of each person needing help. Unfortunately, there's no ready measurement.

The nature of the problem will determine more than anything else how much exploring needs to be done into the various components of a person's background. Ask of the person what you need to know, but only what you need to know. Imagine to yourself that you and the person needing help are drawing a map together. The purpose of the map is to give him specific and accurate directions toward the bridge which has the services he needs on the other side. The map should lead from his needs directly to services. Your understanding of him and of people in general will determine just how well that map is drawn.

BIBLIOGRAPHY

Chiang, Hung-Min and Maslow, Abraham H, eds. *The Healthy Personality: Readings.* New York: Van Nostrand Reinhold, 1969.

Cronbach, Lee J. *Essentials of Psychological Testing.* 2nd ed. New York: Harper, 1960.

Erikson, Erik. *Childhood and Society.* 2nd ed. New York: W.W. Norton and Co, 1963.

———. *Identity: Youth and Crisis.* New York: W.W. Norton and Co, 1968.

Fromm, Erich. *Man for Himself.* New York: Holt, Rhinehart, Winston, 1947.

Hall, Calvin S. and Lindzey, Gardner. *Theories of Personality.* 2nd ed. New York: John Wiley and Sons, 1970.

Harris, Thomas. *I'M OK–You're OK.* New York: Harper and Row, 1967.

Lidz, Theodore. *The Person: His Development Throughout the Life Cycle.* New York: Basic Books, 1968.

Nichtern, Sol. *Helping the Retarded Child.* New York: Grossett and Dunlop, 1974.

Perlman, Helen Harris. *Persona: Social Role and Responsibility.* Chicago: University of Chicago Press, 1968.

Redlich, Fredrick C. and Freedman, Daniel X. *The Theory and Practice of Psychiatry.* New York: Basic Books, 1966.

White, William H. *The Organization Man.* New York: Simon and Schuster, 1956.

chapter seven

Working with People

Helping is a vital part of being human. Everybody, at one time or another, needs help. At other times, we all give help. In fact, we might still be living in caves if we hadn't learned to help each other! A commitment to *mutual aid* has spurred human progress and accounts for our enjoying a standard of living today that our ancestors never dreamed was possible.

In the old days, people were producers, not consumers. They built their homes; grew their food; sewed their clothes; and lived in large families that worked together to meet their basic needs. Such self-sufficient families simply don't exist anymore. As life has become more complicated with the advancement of technology and knowledge, people have had to purchase most of the products and services they need. At the same time, helping has become more complicated, too. Today, a neighbor's helping hand is often not enough. More than the informal assistance of the man next door is sometimes needed in order for a person to get the services and goods he requires to meet his needs and achieve a more satisfying life. The development of the human services in our society is a response to the recognition that professional helping should be available to people who aren't able to secure all they need by themselves.

There are lots of ways of helping people. All of them involve a number of basic components: *people, place, problem, purpose, process,* and *outcome.* Successful helping is determined by the way in which the people involved relate to each other and work towards the solution of the problem confronting them. Professional helping is by no means an easy task. We know that people are complex and often their problems are too. Professional helping should always be guided by asking the question, "What is helpful?"

An action or service is helpful when it solves a problem for a person in order to:

- **meet his basic needs**
- **maintain his dignity**
- **bring him comfort or satisfaction**
- **teach him new problem-solving skills and**
- **encourage his personal growth.**

Obviously, being helpful requires a great deal of skill and knowledge if it is to accomplish any of these goals. We all know what helping means, but we don't always know how to be helpful.

WHAT IS A HELPING PERSON?

A sincere interest in being helpful is certainly important, but rarely enough in successful helping. The helping person must have a number of personal attitudes and attributes which will enable her to be of help to another person. Beginning with a commitment to helping, the helpful person should be able to: listen with understanding and act with skill, experience, information, and self-awareness.

The helping person will present herself in a way that shows her to be an individual who is: warm, interested, caring, optimistic, tolerant, genuine, nonjudgmental, trustworthy, empathetic, responsive, and action-oriented. She will also show the person she is helping that she has a fundamental respect for his basic dignity and worth as a fellow human being. The helping person understands herself and is able to put her own needs aside in order to focus completely on the person who needs her help. She has her own style of relating to people and uses it in helping. She doesn't play any false roles and she is comfortable with her limits as well as her assets. For example, she is able to say, "I don't know" very honestly and not assume that she, the helping person, must be all-knowing. She can also admit there are some things she cannot accomplish for the person she is trying to help. There are times when, despite her best efforts, some goals are not achievable. A good helping person knows this and doesn't undermine herself when she can't be all-giving or "all things to all people."

The helping person also has a high degree of objectivity. She is able to see a situation clearly and does not become emotionally over-identified with the person she is trying to help. Nor does she "take her work home with her" and worry endlessly over work-related problems to such an extent that she cannot enjoy other parts of her life. Helpers who are so invested in their work that nothing else in their lives gets any attention are often the people who "burn out" and become unable to help anyone effectively, including themselves.

Professional competence is, of course, just as important in helping as self-awareness. The competent helper has "done her homework." She has a firm knowledge base regarding people and their problems, personality dynamics, and social systems from which to draw the necessary information she will use in being helpful. In addition to this, she has attained a body of knowledge specifically related to providing human services, such as interviewing techniques. Furthermore, she is aware that her professional education is ongoing, both in classrooms and on-the-job. She is commited to improving her professional competence throughout her career by continuing to learn more about people's needs and motivations, professional skills, and herself.

The helping person is well aware that helping is never a spectator sport. Both the helper and the person receiving help must be actively involved in the process, if it is to be successful. She knows she is working *with*, not *for*, the person who needs help. She isn't "Ms. Fix-it." The person she is helping has a right and a responsibility to be maximally involved in the helping process. Like the consumer of any other service, the person requesting help must decide whether he wants the help that is being offered and whether he believes it will be useful to him. The helping person respects this decision and doesn't impose her preferences or value judgments. To do so would be neither helpful nor appropriate. It is the person seeking help who must ultimately make the decisions and do much of the work to gain help. The helping person is an *enabler* whose activities should always be in harmony with the interests and wishes of the person she is trying to help. Even with those individuals, such as the profoundly retarded or senile whose capacities for decision-making and self-direction are very limited, the helping person will always try to involve them in the helping work, to the extent of their capabilities.

THE HELPING PROCESS

The People • There are always at least two people involved in the helping process: they are the helper and the person needing help. Sometimes, whole families may be involved with a helper. At other times, one person may need several helpers for related, but distinct problems. Usually, however, helping takes place between two individuals. Each of them are unique and come to the helping process with different backgrounds, perceptions, and life experiences. They are usually strangers to each other. In order for helping to occur, they must get to know one another and agree on a cooperative plan of action to achieve help.

The relationship established between the two people is the cornerstone of helping. Whether an individual is requesting help in finding a job or improving his marriage, he will establish some kind of relationship with the helper. The nature of the problem and the amount of interaction between the two people will determine the depth and direction of their helping relationship.

The helping relationship is different from a friendship, a family tie, or any other personal or business involvement. The helping relationship is established with a specific purpose in mind. It is time-limited and expected to last only as long as it takes to accomplish the helping task. Also, the people involved are on somewhat of an unequal footing. There is no room in the helping relationship for extended, aimless small-talk or for the helper to reveal her needs or involve the other person in her daily life. All the attention and activity is centered on the person needing help. His needs form the focus of the relationship and have, in fact, brought it into being.

The helping relationship is the communication bridge between two people that will enable them to gain help effectively. Like all relationships, it requires hard work and a willingness on the part of both people involved to make some investment of themselves. In addition to communication and commitment, a helping relationship requires that the two people involved are able to trust one another as well as understand one another. They must also feel an easy give-and-take between them, an openness in the way they talk to one another. They must share a responsibility for the work at hand if they are to accomplish their helping goal.

In most relationships, the people involved tend to share some common ground. Most of us choose friends who think like us, share our perspectives, have had similar backgrounds, and sometimes even look like us. This is not the way a helping relationship is formed. As often as not, the person seeking help may be of an entirely different ethnic or cultural background, with many life experiences and orientations quite different from our own. Some of my colleagues in the human services discount the importance of the differences between the helper and the person seeking help. They usually say that professional skill will overcome such differences of background and experience. While it is certainly true that a trained worker should be able to establish a productive relationship with an individual who is not a carbon copy of herself, it would be a huge mistake to ignore these differences. For example, I am blonde and blue-eyed. For me to assume that I know what it feels like to be black would be just plain foolish. Nor do I expect a black person to understand what it means to have been raised as a Norwegian-American!

If the people in a helping relationship are to truly understand one another, they must both accept the fact that the total of their backgrounds and identities are involved in the helping process. No human services worker can claim "color blindness" in the relationship without diminishing the person she's trying to help. Where then is the "common ground"? It is to be found in the mutual respect that develops between the two people in the relationship. As they get to know one another, they learn to respect each other as individuals, *including* (not ignoring) whatever sociocultural or economic status differences may exist between them. Respect is the key also to being helpful to a person you don't particularly like. Those workers who say they like everybody are simply not being honest with themselves. In the course of our careers we will all come across people whose personalities we may find unpleasant or boring or even obnoxious. These people are entitled to help, too. After all, they aren't coming to you to win any popularity contests; they need help. If you can push aside your initial reactions and get in touch with your fundamental respect for them as human beings with rights to service, you will be able to be helpful. Whether or not you are ever able to reevaluate your opinion of their personalities is really inconsequential.

The Problem • There are probably as many problems as there are people in the world. And, during your career in human services you are likely to come across a lot of them. However, pinning down just what the problem is sometimes isn't easy. What may be a calamity for one person may hardly bother another. What may be a crisis of overwhelming proportions for one person may not be nearly so devastating for another. A person's inner and outer capacities will determine the severity of some problems in his life. But, however much people's reactions to their problems may vary, the problems themselves are, by definition, creating some amount of difficulty in the individual's life.

Problems, of course, bring with them stress, conflict, and discomfort. When they overtax an individual's coping and problem-solving capacities, he must have help in resolving them and turns to a human services worker. It then becomes the worker's responsibility to clearly define the extent and nature of the problem confronting the individual. Frequently, a problem may be rather simple and straightforward. For example, a senior citizen may need help in securing a new Medicaid card. Just as often, however, investigating the problem may reveal that it is really multidimensional. For example, the worker may find that the senior citizen has not only lost his Medicaid card, but has no money for food and is totally isolated from other people in the community and very depressed and lonely. It is important that a worker try to examine not only the immediate problem, but also the underlying and contributing problems that may be present in a person's life. This does not mean that we go looking for trouble. If the senior citizen wants no additional help, other than the new card, that is his right. Nevertheless, it remains the worker's responsibility to have a comprehensive understanding of the situation so she can offer other appropriate services. She may suggest to the senior citizen that he is eligible for supplementary public assistance or tell him about a local community center where he might enjoy meeting other people his age. He may turn down these service offerings, but at least the worker fulfilled her responsibility to identify and respond to other, related areas in the man's life that might be unsatisfying.

The worker must remember that people perceive problems differently and we, as professionals should not impose personal assessments on the situation. We must rely on the person seeking help to explain to us what the problem is, *as he sees it*. Whether or not we surmise that the real problems lies elsewhere, we must start with the person's evaluation of the situation and its stress-points. Later in the helping process when the relationship has grown is the time to offer another interpretation of the situation, if one exists. In the beginning, it is best to stick to the facts and the problem, as described by the person at the outset.

The Purpose • All helping efforts share a common goal: to bring about some kind of *change*. The nature of the problem will determine where change must occur. Sometimes our task will be to accomplish some change in the person's environment. At other times, we will try to help the person change one of his own attitudes or behaviors. And, at still other times, it may be essential for changes to occur in both these directions in order to solve the problem.

Generally, we seek to bring about change in order to enable the person we are helping to have an opportunity for:

- more satisfying living
- better general functioning
- increased information, and/or
- better self-awareness

Because we are working *with*, not just *for* the person we are helping, our overall goals must include helping him to gain increased skill in problem-solving and in maintaining satisfying interpersonal relationships. Helping should always result in giving a person an increased capacity for more effective living and for self-determination regarding his life pursuits and goals.

A useful tool for determining the purpose of the helping task and for outlining each person's responsibilities in the work is the establishment of a *contract*. Although the helping contract is not a written or legally-binding document, it is an agreement by two people about their expectations of one another in a given situation. Early in the helping relationship, the two people begin to negotiate their contract by discussing and deciding on answers to such questions as:

- **What is the problem?**
- **How can it be solved?**
- **What responsibilities will each one take towards solving the problem?**

Over a period of time, while two people are engaged in the helping process, their contract may have to be renegotiated. They may find that there are additional problems to be worked on together or they may want to find a different approach to solving the first problem. Whether negotiating the original contract or subsequent ones, it should be remembered that both parties are active participants and have the right not to agree to the contract's terms, if found unsuitable. On the one hand, if the person seeking help does not feel able to take certain steps which the helping person says are necessary, then the person seeking help can refuse to go on with the process. On the other hand, if the request for help involves activity by the helping person which she considers inappropriate, she can refuse to accept responsibility for this part of the request. Usually, however, contracts can be established which are agreeable and tolerable to all persons involved, if the helping person is attuned to the needs, abilities, and limitations of the person she wants to help.

In the course of contract making, some decision should be made also about the timing of the helping process. Both persons should agree whether they foresee a brief investment of time (such as one or two contacts) or whether they feel they will need to work together over a longer period. This cannot always be accurately predicted, of course, but an effort should be made to get some general idea about how long and how frequently the two people will meet to work on the problem.

The Process • The helping process is essentially a learning experience that engages two people in problem-solving through the use of two helping tools: (1) *the relationship* and (2) *the interview*. Human services workers often feel far more comfortable about establishing helping relationships than they do about attempting interviews. Interviewing needn't be so mysterious or anxiety-provoking. After all, you interview people all the time in the course of a typical day. We all ask questions, respond to information, and try to learn about things all day long. That's what goes on in an interview, too.

An interview is more than just conversation. During an interview, the helping person is involved in *listening, observing, questioning,* and *acting*. Through each of these activities, she is attempting to learn enough about the person and his problem so that she can be helpful.

Listening is a special art. Unfortunately, most of us spend a lot more time talking than we do listening to each other. In professional helping, listening should have equal importance with talking and acting. There is much to be learned by listening. First and foremost, we need to listen to the person asking for help in order to learn:

- **what he sees as his problem**
- **what he thinks needs to be done about it**
- **what he has already tried to do about it and**
- **what he expects the helper to be able to do about it**

By listening both to the verbal and the non-verbal messages a person gives, we can learn about a person and his problem. We can come to know:

- **how the person sees himself (as a winner or loser)**
- **how he sees his world (as fearful, fun, etc.)**
- **what his life goals are or whether he has any**
- **how he sees other people (as enjoyable or threatening)**
- **how he copes with life or defends himself against it**
- **what help means to him and**
- **what life is really like for him**

Professional helpers learn to listen with what has been called *a third ear*. They listen to what the person says and also to what he means and what he does. They are sensitive to picking up inconsistencies between a person's stated intentions and his actions, and they listen with understanding to the meaning behind such discrepancies. The following story illustrates the point.

Rosie was a little girl with whom I'd been working for a few months. Shortly after Christmas, while we were taking a walk, one of her schoolmates came along and the two girls began to compare notes on their Christmas presents. As it became clear that the other child had gotten bigger and better presents, Rosie announced that she had received a piano. That ended the competition and the other girl was duly impressed. When the other child had gone on her way, I was tempted to tell Rosie that I knew perfectly well she hadn't gotten any piano. Instead I said, "You really wish you'd gotten a piano, don't you?" From there we were able to talk about what the piano meant to her and why it was so important to win the one-upsmanship game with her classmate. The "third ear" made a big difference being able to understand Rosie and ultimately help her.

The helping person must also listen for what is left unsaid. Sometimes people omit from their discussion the very things that are most important, and sometimes most painful, to them. In fact, people's silences are in themselves important. New workers often feel uncomfortable with people's silences and are overeager for the talk to begin again. Silences should be permitted whenever necessary. Some people need silence as a "breathing space" during which they reflect on what has just been said, or take time to decide what to say next, or calm down, or do whatever else may be needed before they can continue talking about themselves or their problems. A worker must recognize and allow for this. Only when silences are excessive and often repeated must the worker begin to try to dissolve them. Usually, however, silences should be accepted as part of the normal rhythm of interviews.

Observing is the partner of listening and is an important key in understanding. In addition to observing the patterns in an individual's behavioral responses, his body language will communicate a great deal to the skilled observer. There are many elements of body language to note:

clothing	physique	posture
tension	facial expression	eye contact
tone of voice	touching	distance
head movements	gestures	speech patterns

The non-verbal messages given through body language will reveal a great deal about a person's feelings and attitudes. These non-verbal signals can either reinforce or contradict a person's verbal statements. If, for example, a housewife tells you that everything is wonderful and she feels great, but her clothes are in wrinkles, her tone of voice is depressed, her posture makes her look as if she can barely hold herself up, and her eyes are deeply sad, you should be able to tell that all is not well, even if the woman can't say so with words. Knowledge of body language is another indicator of how a person feels about himself and his situation which can be quite useful in interviewing and in helping.

Questioning is another important part of interviewing. All interviewing questions should be designed to do one or all of the following:

- **help the other person to express and understand his feelings and attitudes about his problem**

- **provide the helping person with sufficient information about the nature of the problem and the other person's abilities so that an effective problem-solving strategy can be developed**

- **provide the other person with the opportunity to learn and master new problem-solving techniques**

The questions should also be constructed in such a way as to make them clear and readily understandable. Then, too they should be open-ended, rather than closed, encouraging descriptive, rather than one-word (i.e., yes or no) answers. The worker needs to be sensitive enough to the person's emotional state and defenses to keep from injecting "loaded" questions into an interview prematurely. Nothing useful can be accomplished by doing this and often in fact it will have a very negative effect on the helping relationship. If for example, a person is not ready to tell you about his secret drinking, there is absolutely nothing to be gained by confronting him with a question, such as, "Are you an alcoholic?"

However well-constructed the questions, they should never be asked in a rapid-fire barrage. Even when you need certain pieces of information rather quickly, it is more useful to invite the person to tell you about himself than to overwhelm him with "20 questions." If you are listening carefully to what you are being told, observing the person you are talking to, and asking only needed, open questions you will surely be able to acquire substantial amounts of information.

One other aspect of questioning is extremely important. The helping person's questions are always limited to asking only for information that is directly relevant to the problem-solving task at hand. It is never in order for a worker to indulge her curiosity or infringe on another person's privacy casually. All of us have the right to keep our feelings and thoughts to ourselves, if we so choose. Nor are we compelled to share information about ourselves and our lives if we prefer not to, except in court testimony. If we really respect the person we are trying to help, we will respect his right to privacy as much as possible. In situations where the person refuses to tell us enough so that we can be helpful, we have a responsibility to tell him that we can't help unless he provides certain specific pieces of information. Should he then choose not to do so and help, consequently, isn't possible, that is unfortunate, but it is the person's right.

Acting, on the part of the helping person, should always be intentional and purposeful. In addition to carefully listening and observing and to asking skillful questions, the helping person makes many responses to the other person in the course of an interview. All of them are thoughtful and should be undertaken with the goal of bringing the helping task closer to a successful conclusion. There are numerous responses that can be made during a helping interview, including:

supporting	explaining	informing
advising	agreeing	disagreeing
reviewing	preparing	reinforcing
confronting	clarifying	reassuring

At one time or another, during the helping relationship, it is likely that the helper will employ most, if not all of these techniques. There is no set of hard-and-fast rules to apply in determining which response is best at a given moment in an interview. The helping person will be guided by her ability to accurately assess the situation and the person she is helping. Just as it is wrong to offer false reassurances to a person we are helping, it would also be wrong to expect a beginning human services worker to have an intuitive grasp of situations and a well-developed repertoire of appropriate responses. Responding effectively is a learned art; one that is acquired through experience and through trial-and-error.

Responding effectively does not mean that the helping person shouldn't be spontaneous. Do your best to promote a good relationship; listen with understanding; and respond authentically. After the interview, reexamine what went on and recall what happened between the two of you. Carefully and objectively look at your own responses, with a critical eye. By doing this you will be able to see what responses may have led you both off the track from problem-solving, and what responses were helpful in creating a climate of trust and movement toward problem-solving. However, if during the interview, you become too preoccupied with "staging" your responses and anticipating what the other person will say or do next, the interview will be unproductive for both of you.

Sometimes your responses will need to be very short ones. These responses can be called "go-ons" because they are intended to communicate to the other person that he should go on with what he has been telling you. When a person seems reluctant to go on, you can signify your continuing interest by nodding your head affirmatively, by restating his last words, or by saying "um-hum" in a tone that invites his further communication. Because he ultimately has the answers to solving the problem, it is far more important that you encourage him to talk rather than talking yourself.

Responding to a person's statements, requests, feelings, and situations should be guided by an assessment of what will be helpful to him. The helping person strives to be sensitive to the other's needs at all times during interviews. She has this empathic understanding to guide her in asking questions and making responses that will be appropriate and helpful, not threatening or anxiety-arousing.

Unhelpful Responses

Each helping person must use the total of her personality and skill in order to be helpful. It is not possible to blueprint helpful responses. There are, however, a number of responses that are generally *un*helpful. They include:

1 • **Making such statements as, "Pull yourself together," "Cheer up," or "You shouldn't feel that way." (If a person could solve his problem independently and make himself feel better in the process, he wouldn't be asking for help.)**

2 • **Using put-downs or sarcasm to motivate someone. (The person is there for help, not criticism.)**

3   ● Giving commands; "You should do this; should not do that" (While it is often helpful to suggest alternatives, it is helping no one to be coldly commanding.)

4   ● Making judgments, i.e., "You never. . . ." (The use of absolutes has no place in helping. Never say never.)

5   ● Feigning understanding. (Only say "I understand" when you really do. If you don't, be humble enough to ask for clarification.)

6   ● Jumping to conclusions. (It is presumptuous to assume that anyone can size up a situation or a person without careful consideration. Real understanding takes time.)

7   ● Enforcing your timetable. (Progress never follows a straight line. Neither does helping. And, it should take place at the other person's pace, not yours.)

8   ● Rambling—either yours or the other person's. (Though small talk may be initially useful to break the ice, too much meaningless, undirected discussion later on can only dilute the relationship and the possibility of helping.)

9   ● Waking all sleeping dogs. (The contract has defined the work. It is not appropriate to try to uncover every problem in a person's personality or life. Some sleeping dogs should be left alone.)

10   ● Allowing excessive dependency. (It is one thing to allow the other person to borrow some of your strength and rely on you for help in problem-solving. It is quite another—and always unhelpful—to allow him to abdicate decision-making over his own life in your favor.)

The helping process is a skillful blend of listening, questioning, and responding. Throughout the process the helping person will be continually assessing the other individual's motivations, capacities, and opportunities. She will also be focusing on his strengths. Many new workers forget that it is the person's strengths that are of utmost importance in the helping process. As a beginning worker, I too busily engaged myself in the "pathology hunt." Somehow I thought that the more pathology I could uncover in a person or his life situation, the more evidence there was of my professional competence. I certainly had things backwards, didn't I? Enabling a person to build on his strengths so his capacity to solve his problems will increase and his life will be more satisfying is the goal of helping. It's easy enough, with some training, to find at least a little something pathological in everybody. So what? To do so may be fascinating, but it's rarely very helpful. Look instead for strengths. Encourage the person you're helping to develop them. *That's* helping!

The Place • Helping can take place anywhere—in a home, at an office, on a street corner, or even by telephone. Wherever two people meet to work together on a problem, helping can take place.

Most helping is accomplished through interviews in an office. The office itself—its decorations and other characteristics—can be helpful or not, depending on whether it is conducive to concentration on problem-solving without unnecessary distractions or interruptions. A good interviewing room is one which is comfortable and quiet, free of clutter or ornamentation that will call attention away from the problem-solving work.

Although some workers prefer to sit behind a desk with the other person facing them, the professional distance implied by this unequal arrangement detracts from its helpfulness. Probably the best arrangement is for both people to sit near each other, at slight angles in comfortable chairs, providing good eye contact. The room should also have available ashtrays and kleenex as well as adequate lighting and heating. If possible, the room should be sound-proofed and a "do not disturb" sign hung on the door to insure maximum privacy.

While office interviews are often preferred because they are considered "neutral ground," some individuals may be unwilling or unable to come to an office for the help they need. For them, home visits are helpful. Home visits are also indicated when it is important to learn more about a person's actual living arrangement or family relationships. Many people feel more comfortable talking about their problems in the security of their own homes. However, it is also true that some people find it more difficult to "get down to business" when they are there, preferring to play host or hostess. The helping person should be aware of these possibilities and discuss them with the other individual. It is also useful to ask him how he feels about having company.

Home visits can yield a great deal of information which will be useful in helping, if the helping person is mindful of observing quietly what the home looks like and what it tells about the other person. The helper needn't expect a "guided tour," however. Unless the problem concerns some aspect of the home itself, it is unnecessary for her to conduct an inspection of the grounds. The helper is there to work, not to be treated like a guest.

During home visits, refreshments are often offered. A polite refusal is usually appropriate. Again, the helper hasn't come to be served like a guest. If, however, the person you're visiting has prepared something especially for you, don't offend him by refusing. Just tell him later that it really isn't necessary for him to make anything for you the next time you come.

Both home visits and office interviews should be time-limited. Usually, an interview should go on for no longer than forty-five to fifty minutes. It is difficult for either person to sustain their concentration for good discussion after that. Of course, it is possible that everything between them can be said in a shorter amount of time, on some occasions. When this happens and it is decided not to begin discussing something else that day, there is nothing wrong with concluding the interview at a natural point rather than stretching it to fill up a predetermined time space.

When interviews are conducted on the telephone or in other surroundings, it is more difficult to apply either a time-limit or other structure. However, as with in-person interviews, talking to someone on the telephone should be considered a process similar to any other interview. This is true for those situations when help is requested in any other set of circumstances. Listening, questioning, and responding can obviously take place in open spaces as well as anywhere else.

The Outcome • Hopefully, the end result of the helping process will be the accomplishment of some change in a person's life which he considers helpful. The change has come about by your joint efforts at problem-solving. When change is achieved, the helping process is nearly complete. The only work yet to be done is to end the helping relationship and for each person to come away from the experience better equipped to problem-solve in the future.

Helping could be viewed as a process within a process. In addition to the sequence of activities already discussed—establishing a relationship, listening, questioning, and responding—the entire helping process has a life of its own: a beginning, a middle, and an ending.

The beginning of the helping process is the phase during which the helping person and the person seeking help begin to establish their relationship through exploring the problem at hand. During this period, they also develop their contract. They decide on the best action strategy for handling and resolving the problem and they agree on their respective roles and responsibilities for getting the work done.

The middle of the helping process is the "getting down to business" time. During this phase, priorities in the problem-solving are established and followed by breaking down the problem, if necessary, in order to attend to one thing at a time. The entire action strategy is eventually implemented and all agreed-on activities for problem-solving are undertaken.

The ending of the helping process is the closing phase when the work has been accomplished and the two people who have worked together must separate. It is also the time for summing the learning experience they have shared and reflecting on the work done. The helping person should skillfully end the helping process. A quick "good-bye" is never enough. Instead, some time should be given to talking about what's been accomplished and proper leave-taking.

The end of the helping process is the time for the helping person to do some careful self-assessment of her activities and accomplishments on the other's behalf. When there has been successful problem resolution, this task is sometimes easier than when your efforts have failed. The task must be undertaken in either event, nevertheless, if the helper is to grow professionally through her experiences.

Professional helping isn't easy. It isn't easy for the person needing help either. In our society, a high value is placed on independent functioning and self-sufficiency. Asking for help means somewhat the opposite and that is hard for any of us to accept, at times. Helping is complicated by the fact that people can often be their own worst enemies. They may need help, but not necessarily want it. If there is one ultimate truth in this life, it is probably the fact that *timing is all-important.* No matter how good our intentions, if a person isn't ready for help, little can be given. But, even when the results aren't immediately visible, I don't think any helping effort is in vain. Through your efforts, a person may well be able to accept help and use it later, when the timing is better for him.

Professional helping is sometimes short-circuited by the very social systems that have been created to help people in our society.

The helping person trying to engage them on the other's behalf may achieve bureaucratic obstacles, red-tape and frustration instead of help in her efforts. In the next chapter, effective working with systems in order to achieve help for people will be discussed more fully.

Finally, professional helping isn't a simple matter because it is no easy task to learn what the other guy's shoes feel like. Nor is it easy, once having learned, to use yourself effectively on his behalf. But, don't give up. With every helping experience, your skill will grow. If you maintain an ongoing commitment to increasing your professional skill, your knowledge base, and your self-awareness through objective self-appraisal, you will, indeed be helpful to others.

BIBLIOGRAPHY

Benjamin, Alfred. *The Helping Interview.* Boston: Houghton Mifflin, 1969.

Brill, Naomi. *Working with People: the Helping Process.* Philadelphia: Lippincott, 1973.

Egan, Gerard. *The Skilled Helper: A Model for Systematic Helping and Interpersonal Relating.* Monterey, California: Brooks/Cole, 1975.

Garrett, Annette. *Interviewing: Its Principles and Methods.* 2nd ed. New York: Family Service Assn. of America, 1972.

Johnson, David W. *Reaching Out: Interpersonal Effectiveness and Self-Actualization.* Englewood Cliffs, N.J.: Prentice-Hall, Inc., 1972.

Schubert, Margaret. *Interviewing in Social Work Practice.* New York: Council on Social Work Education, 1971.

Whittaker, James. *Social Treatment: An Approach to Interpersonal Helping.* Chicago: Aldine, 1974.

chapter eight

Working with Systems

The dominant goal of the human services is to meet people's needs more fully, more effectively, and more efficiently. To achieve this goal, the human services must make society's social systems work for people. And, in order to activate systems to be of greater benefit for people, it is essential that the human services worker gain a familiarity with systems—how they operate, how they can be influenced and/or utilized, how they can be coordinated, and how, if need be, they can be changed.

SOCIAL SYSTEMS

The preceding chapter has focused on work with individuals. It is equally important for the student of human services to acquire a beginning expertise in working with social systems. There are numerous social systems with which the human services worker is engaged on a daily basis. For example: a family, a therapy group, a block association, a professional organization, a community, and a bureaucracy are all called social systems. In fact, each time a worker is involved with several people instead of an individual, she is working with a system.

We spend most of our waking hours relating and responding to many social systems. The sociologists have told us that human beings are "social animals." We thrive on contact with others and react negatively to extended isolation. We live in communities for this reason, too. We are clearly and increasingly *interdependent*. Civilization's unfolding and all human progress are the result of people's cooperative efforts. The development of each of us as individuals parallels the growth of civilization. None of us would have become a functioning person if it hadn't been for the efforts of others to enable us to grow physically, socially, and emotionally. Our parents, extended family, peers, teachers, neighbors and many significant others gave us the opportunity to become who we are. By the same token, our efforts on behalf of other people will in some way have impact on their development.

Mutual aid, from which we all benefit, implies *reciprocity*. We know that "for every action there is a reaction." This is just as true in the human services as it is in physics. The key to effective human services intervention is the ability to stimulate an action which will trigger the desired reaction needed to solve a problem. Since most of the problems people bring to human services workers are caused by the environment, the workers must be able to somehow change the negative impact of the environment with and for the people they are trying to help. Obviously, the enormous complexity and heterogeneity of our modern, rather impersonalized society makes it difficult to determine the right action for the right reaction. It takes a bit of detective work and a solid knowledge of alternatives to achieve the right combination. In every instance, it also requires successful working with systems.

Working with systems can have multiple purposes and goals, in various situations. On the other hand, a system can become a client/patient. This is so when a worker is engaged with a group. The group is the client with whom the worker attempts to problem solve. On the other hand, the worker may be required to initiate activity with a larger system (such as a hospital, school, or welfare bureaucracy) on behalf of an individual client or a client group. Whichever type of systems work is undertaken, the human services worker is constantly fulfilling her primary function as a *bridge* between people and systems.

WORKING WITH GROUPS

An understanding of group dynamics is fundamental to effective intervention by a human services worker. Following is an introductory explanation of working with groups. However, the human services student is encouraged to pursue this skill much further than the limits of this book.

There are all kinds of groups: teams, families, classes, clubs, councils, staffs, peers, committees, gangs, and trade unions, to name a few. Groups can be educational, recreational, therapeutic, or action-oriented. In every group, regardless of its size, shape, or reason for establishment, there is reciprocity between the members and some degree of mutual aid occurring. People join groups in order to accomplish something they want or need.

A person may join his community group because he agrees with their efforts to get better street lights in the neighborhood. He may join a chess club because he is interested in the pure enjoyment of the game and expects to find challenging partners among the other members. He may join the union at work because he believes the union representatives will fight for his interests. And, he may simultaneously join a therapy group because he is feeling uncomfortable in his more intimate relationships and anticipates that by participating in this group he will achieve better interpersonal skills. In each of these examples, the person chose to join a group because he felt that his interests and needs could be better met by his involvement with a system or group, rather than with a single individual.

A group is considered an entity itself. It is, in a sense, larger than the sum of its parts because it is a more effective vehicle for accomplishing certain tasks than any of its individual members could be on their own. Groups are vital to effective human services efforts, just as they are to us in the normal course of our daily lives.

Group Process

Not all groups attempt to deal with "problems" necessarily. Many are established simply to provide members with enjoyment and recreational outlets. Sometimes human services workers will be interested in developing such groups, i.e., for teenagers or senior citizens. Usually, however, there is a purposeful intent on the worker's part to plan and implement the development of a group for one of two basic service-connected reasons:

1 • **To stimulate satisfying programs and/or actions to secure the attainment of some goal in the larger environment (i.e., to get street lights) or**

2 • **To address personal problems in living which are shared by a number of individuals (i.e., therapy)**

A human services worker may regularly be called upon to be a group leader for individuals seeking to meet together to work on either (or both) of the above goals. To be an effective and helpful leader, the worker takes responsibility for understanding how people function in groups and how the group itself functions and develops.

Each group has characteristics unique to that particular membership and each group has a special life of its own. Yet, every group has some similar dynamics and follows an identifiable process in its unfolding. There are many variables that distinguish one group from another. The most significant are: the group's purpose, the group's composition, and the group's structure and functioning.

The group's purpose may be the accomplishment of a stated goal through working together on clearly defined tasks, i.e., a group of parents may join together to hold a bazaar which will earn money for new playground equipment. Or, the group's purpose may be more open-ended, created to provide the members with an opportunity to talk over and work through their individual problems together, i.e., a therapy group. In both situations, the purpose of the group will largely effect the size and shape of its membership. And, the group's purpose and membership together will influence significantly the operation and outcome of the group and its success in achieving its goals.

If a group's purpose is clearly task-oriented towards solving a problem in the larger environment, it is usually helpful to encourage the participation of many people and to permit the group's membership to be large. It is obvious that neither labor unions nor block associations nor other community groups would be very successful if they weren't able to recruit a sizable and visible constituency to reinforce their demands. In large groups, there is likely to be much diversity among the membership regarding ages, backgrounds, attitudes, and personalities. In a therapeutically-oriented group, however, this type of group generally cannot be overly large or include people who are so very different in personality that they cannot relate well to one another. A therapy group usually is comprised of not more than ten individuals who have at least some personal difficulty in common and who can readily identify, at least to some limited extent, with the other group members.

In every group, there is work to be done—something to be accomplished. The group's success or lack of success will be determined not only by the relevance of their stated goal and the personality characteristics of the members, but also will, in large measure, be determined by the structure of the group, the degree of unity within it, and the manner in which it moves towards its goals. The group's structure here refers to the roles and relationships established among members, as well as the responsibilities each member is willing to assume to further the group's interests. The structure also includes the time the members spend together and the regularity and continuity of their group meetings.

It is generally important that groups establish a regular meeting time (such as once a week or once a month) and that the meeting time be used specifically and exclusively for pursuing the group's defined purposes. The functioning of every group can best be evaluated by scrutinizing the activities of the group, and the regularity of those activities in the pursuit of its goals. For example, an assessment of whether or not each member of an action-oriented group has carried out the responsibilities he has accepted is one way to measure the group's solidarity and stability. Another measure for any kind of group is attendance. If people are attending only sporadically it may be that the group is not satisfying its members' needs as promised. If a group is progressing well, it is likely that its members will be sharing an identity with the group, a high level of interest in its work, and a sense of cohesion with the other members. In most groups, however, such straight-line progress doesn't "just happen" spontaneously. It requires a leader's skill and involvement.

Self-Help Groups

There is one relatively new kind of group that is growing in popularity and utility to the human services. This is the *self-help group*. There are numerous such groups which are established for the benefit of individuals who share a common problem in living. Alcoholics Anonymous is probably the most famous self-help group.

There are many other groups, such as: abusive parents, gamblers, widows, cardiac patients, or overeaters. While each of these groups makes an invaluable contribution to the human services, they share a commitment to remaining totally without direct professional leadership in their group efforts. These self-help groups are led and maintained by their members, who have chosen to exclude professionals from leadership roles. Professionals should not be insulted, there's plenty of other work for them and the self-help groups are doing a good job for their members that merits the respect of the professional community. Because of their proven usefulness, it is important for the human services worker to not only know of the existence of local self-help groups, but to have specific information available so that she may refer an individual to such a group when she believes that individual could benefit from their efforts.

Except for the self-help group, the human services worker may be called on to lead almost any kind of group. When in the role of group leader, the human services worker is similar to the conductor of an orchestra. The leader is hopefully adept at blending the member's efforts and contributions into effective, harmonious action.

Leading a Group

The worker's role in leading a group shares many similarities to her role in interviewing a single individual. She is guided in both situations by the overall goal of promoting or enhancing her clients' functioning and satisfaction in daily living. She is working with them to maximize their potential for gratifying living and their competence at problem-solving. To achieve these goals, she uses the principal interviewing techniques mentioned earlier: *listening, observing, questioning,* and *acting.*

When working with groups, the worker's job is simultaneously doubled and divided. Because a group is a multiclient situation, the worker needs to be doubly alert as she listens and observes. Frequently, there will be many interactions taking place at the same time in a group. A worker tries to tune in as widely as possible. Fortunately, she is better enabled to do this because she is not expected to respond to each group member's comments exclusively. Group members also talk as much to each other as to their leader, thereby giving the leader time to observe how the group is functioning. Her role, however, is not by any means limited to passive observations. She is also actively guiding and facilitating the group's goals. To do so, she must ask pertinent, relevant questions of the group in order to develop problem-solving strategies.

The group's first task after its establishment is to decide what its purpose or problem is. The leader provides the members with an opportunity to voice what is bothering them and to suggest how they feel the group might be helpful to them. Once all views are aired, the group must do some sorting and decide what direction to take. It is not uncommon for individuals in a group to have slightly different perceptions of the major problem as well as somewhat differing expectations for what the group can accomplish. These differences need to be talked about so that a *consensus* can be reached among the members. It is vitally important that from the outset the group's objectives—whether specific or general—are clearly defined and agreed upon by the membership.

Developing a Group Contract

It is during this initial period of the group's life, when the members are striving for a consensus about goals, that they are also negotiating their *contract*. A group's contract is like the one negotiated in individual interviews (previously discussed). The contract is similar to a map which charts the course for the group's future directions. Of course as the group evolves, its contract may have to be renegotiated if there is a consensus at a later time that this is needed.

A group follows a developmental process with distinguishable beginning, middle, and ending phases. While many theories of group development exist that cite varying numbers of steps through which a group evolves, the following three phases describe the most pronounced shifts in a group's life.

Beginning Phase • the period in which the group is created, membership drawn, a consensus reached about purpose, a contract negotiated, and orientation shared by the members about the group's structure and function

Middle Phase • the period in which the group experiences a strong sense of cohesiveness and is highly active in pursuing its goals

Ending Phase • the period in which the group's goals have been achieved (or abandoned); a time for assessment of the group's usefulness for its members before a decision is made to dissolve the group

It becomes the responsibility of the worker/leader to make sure that the group with which she is engaged is able to move through all three phases at well-timed intervals. She notes when the beginning work is completed by the group before encouraging them to move along to their middle phase. She also provides encouragement if the group is dawdling through its early getting-acquainted activities. Similarly, the worker helps the group move from its middle "down to business" phase to its completion and "wrapping up" stage before disbanding. It is important that the worker, while being aware that the group is ready for some movement, not coerce the group to change its pace to suit her timetable. The worker will appropriately suggest new emphasis on goal-achievement when it is called for, but the actual decision to move on must be by group consensus. There is always the possibility that the group has a reason for delaying its own progress and that the contract will need to be renegotiated. A worker should raise this possibility with the group members, too.

Throughout a group's existence, the leader has a number of roles and responsibilities:

- **to facilitate clear communication**
- **to provide information and alternatives**
- **to promote problem-solving and constructive action**
- **to protect the group's contract, confidentiality, and ground rules**
- **to modify the environment**
- **to "keep house"**

The worker seeks to establish and maintain clear, open channels of communication within the group by helping the members to find common ground and focus on the group's goals. Borrowing from her repertoire of interviewing techniques, she will guide (not control) the group interactions by raising relevant questions and making observations that will keep the group goal-directed and will encourage the balanced and equal participation of all the group's members.

The group's success at problem-solving will be greatly enhanced by the leader's contributions of information about resources and feasible alternative action strategies, as well as information about obstacles the group should anticipate from a chosen course of action. Again, the leader should not pressure the group into accepting her preferred approach or method of problem-solving. But, she does have a responsibility to help the group to weigh the practicality of their choice of action.

In every instance, the leader should be prepared to encourage and support the group's constructive efforts towards problem-solving. There is no reason for the leader to remain passive or detached about the group's efforts. On the contrary, it is expected that she, too, has a commitment to the group's goals and her enthusiasm over the group's achievement of them is entirely appropriate.

Developing Ground Rules

Every group sets up ground rules for the nature and intensity of its interactions. For example, one therapy group may decide to not permit its members to discuss their respective ancient histories. When this ground rule is broken, the leader should point it out so the group can avoid unnecessary digressions. Ground rules are often included in the group's contract, but sometimes come up later and need to be added. The worker needs to be alert to this possibility and to bring it to the group's attention for discussion and resolution. Her primary concern is protecting the contract; she seeks clarification about ground rules to insure that the latter will not conflict or interfere with efficient problem-solving.

There are several other ground rules that usually apply in all groups. For example, members are generally expected to listen to each other, to respond to each other, to be relevant in their comments, and to give "equal time" to all group members. When these interactional rules are not being followed and are causing friction or discomfort within the group, it is the leader's responsibility to confront the situation and the individual(s) precipitating it so that the group can proceed with its tasks.

There are times when a group leader will find it necessary to engage in work with other, usually larger social systems on her group's behalf. Sometimes, her professional status and influence are needed to give a group an opening to discuss (and hopefully resolve) a problem a system may be creating. Or, the worker may seek some system change for the group without their direct, active involvement. In both cases, the worker is serving as a *bridge* between systems and people. Her intervention is designed to make the systems more responsive to the needs of the people in her group. For example, she may advocate her group's interests with other community organizations or bureaucracies or even with her own agency. Techniques for systems intervention will be discussed more fully later in this chapter.

Because the leader must be a catalyst at times, it is important that she be up-to-date in her "housekeeping" chores. Such duties include: observing members' attendance patterns and interaction patterns, securing a meeting space in advance for group meetings, publicizing and recruiting people for group functions or for membership in the group itself, as well as countless other activities that will facilitate the group's progress. Most of these tasks are self-explanatory. But, special note should be made of the importance of seating arrangements. When working with a very large group of people, it is usually necessary that they be seated in rows. However, for smaller groups where a good deal of interaction is desired, positioning chairs (of equal size) in a circle has proven to be the arrangement most conducive to comfortable discussion.

By now it should be clear that a group leader has many tasks and responsibilities. A group leader is a very busy person, to be sure! Leading a group is similar to a juggling act; a good deal of well-synchronized movements are needed to achieve the goal.

Reading about groups can never be as effective a teaching tool as actually becoming involved and leading one. Just as there are no blueprints for interviewing, none has been developed for leading groups. As always, it falls to the student to absorb as much as possible from classes and text and to integrate that knowledge with practical experience in the field. It has been said that, "There is magic in a group." It's probably more accurate to say that a leader's skill makes it appear so. Skill in leading is acquired through a mixture of alert involvement in the group process, attention to leadership tasks, reflection on the work done and the work undone, practice and more practice, and a dash of trial-and-error.

SYSTEMS SKILLS

Whether leading a group, working with an individual, or dealing with a large, impersonal bureaucracy, the human services worker consistently presents herself, genuinely, to others as *a helping person.* The characteristics of her helpfulness have been discussed more fully in other sections of this book. Here, let's take a look at those skills which are of particular importance in working with systems—be they groups, communities, or bureaucracies.

Whenever a human services worker wishes to guide an individual, family, or action-oriented group toward bringing change by direct confrontation with a larger social system, it is absolutely essential that the worker have some solid knowledge about the target system. Without it, she may well go knocking on the wrong bureaucratic doors and become decidedly unhelpful. The worker's skills should include:

- **knowledge of the community power structure**
- **knowledge of intervention techniques**
- **knowledge of fiscal realities**
- **knowledge of the internal workings of large, complex, formal organizations**

The worker needs to know how the community or city operates—who the public officials are, what the local government agencies are and what they do, what other citizen groups exist, where to go and who to speak to, and how to find appropriate resources. Once she has established which agency or organization it is whose cooperation she must enlist to solve the problem, she must determine how the agency should best be approached.

For example, in a situation where a community group with which a worker is involved wants a school crossing guard stationed at the local elementary school on a daily basis, the worker must first decide which would be the most influential official or government agency to contact. It is usually advisable to make initial contacts with agencies closest to the community. In this instance, the group and the worker should probably try to meet with the captain of the local police precinct to discuss their request. If that doesn't work, they could contact the local assemblyman or congressman representing their community for assistance. Politicians are generally responsive to their constituents in such matters. However, if all else fails, the group may decide to take their problem to city hall or to the media for resolution. Throughout their efforts, they will be guided by the worker's clear understanding of the community's power structure and of the appropriate sequence of pressure points to touch in order to get constructive results.

When a group is taking the initiative in problem-solving, it is generally most useful to speak to the highest authority within the system being confronted, such as a letter to the mayor. However, in situations where the worker alone is negotiating with a particular system on behalf of her individual client or a group, it is often more appropriate for her to "go through channels." It is far more time-consuming than useful for a worker to demand a meeting with the mayor every time a city system has done a disservice to one of her clients. It would be much more productive for the worker to make direct contact with the same person in the system with whom the client himself usually deals.

If, for example, Mr. Olson feels certain he is being short-changed in his welfare budget, the worker can usually make more of an impact by going directly to the welfare investigator involved who is certain to know more about the case than her superiors. An attempt should first be made to enlist this other professional's cooperation in problem-solving for Mr. Olson. If this is not possible, then it is time to climb the agency's professional hierarchy. Since supervisors prefer to speak to other supervisors, the worker appropriately requests her immediate supervisor to make contact at that level. There are occasions when it becomes necessary to go to the top (to the agency director). Even though the original worker is not directly involved, she remains vigilant to insure that some action is being taken. No, she doesn't bombard her boss with reminders. But, she does keep an eye on things and ask her supervisor for feedback. Most situations can usually be handled between the worker herself and a colleague at another agency.

When working with systems, it is becoming increasingly important to know who controls the community purse strings. The worker needs, therefore, to have at least a beginning familiarity with budgets and funding patterns. There are two useful examples to be drawn from the child welfare field to illustrate this.

First, let's assume the worker is engaged with a group of parents of retarded youngsters who are pressing for the development of a group home facility for retarded children in the neighborhood. The group may want to take their demand to the Board of Education. However, the worker knows that such facilities need the approval and funding of a number of agencies within the local government. She should explain that the group's efforts could best be directed toward this approval instead. Without that kind of knowledge, a good deal of effort and impetus for a valuable idea can be dissipated needlessly.

Second, let's assume that the worker is involved with a family whose youngsters had been in foster care briefly a year ago and were now at home. The family is considering asking the foster care agency to help them with Johnny's current behavior problem. The worker knows, however, that the agency is only reimbursed (by government agencies) for providing substitute care when a youngster cannot remain at home. The agency is unable to provide counseling to others, which the worker can explain to the family and save them the time of an inappropriate referral. Then she can proceed to find a child guidance clinic that can help Johnny.

Knowing how an agency or organization is funded will also reveal the source to which it is accountable. Sometimes, to problem-solve effectively, a worker may have to go to that source, if the agency is not performing as it was intended. Of course it would not be appropriate for the human services worker to march into the offices of a philanthropic foundation to complain that the agency to whom they gave money wasn't using it wisely. But, having such information about funding can be useful within the structure of the worker's agency where a joint decision can be made about steps to be taken.

The above examples also emphasize another, less formal role of the human services worker—as a *team player*. Certainly, it is essential for the worker to possess and demonstrate good leadership ability in her efforts with individuals and with systems. Simultaneously, however, she will be demonstrating a capacity to work cooperatively and effectively with other professionals toward their mutual problem-solving goal. There is nothing more boring (or inadequate) than the fellow who is constantly belittling others' helping efforts in his misguided determination to "save the world single-handedly"! Such thinly disguised competitiveness has no place in human services. *Cooperation* is the name of the game.

Negotiating Systems

One of these days, it would not be surprising if an entire course entitled "Negotiating Systems" is added to the human services curriculum. Workers, at all levels and in all subsystems, are finding it necessary to spend more and more time dealing with large social systems and their respective bureaucracies in order to achieve any problem-solving goals. And, the effort is the cause of increasing frustration, to say the least. Blaming a multitude of sins on the "big, bad bureaucracy" or a fouled-up computer is a commonplace explanation these days for unsuccessful problem-solving. While it's true that a mammoth bureaucracy and a poorly-programmed computer can cause monumental mix-ups and obstacles, it is also true that some professionals give up too easily.

In recent years, a healthy awareness has grown that we *can* "fight city hall"—and win. We can also take on the bureaucracy and engage it in problem-solving, *if* we know what we're doing. What we are actually doing in our forays with systems is stimulating *multidimensional helping*. As in every helping effort, there is a process going on. When our work with an individual or group makes it clear that it is essential to involve a larger system in the problem-solving, the worker attempts to bring the system's resources to the individual or group. To do so, she should take three sequential steps:

1 • **Identify the system(s) and resources**

2 • **Link the system(s) with the people**

3 • **Mobilize the system(s) and the people**

First, the worker uses her knowledge of community resources to determine which system(s) will need to be involved in the problem-solving. Then, she creates the *bridge* between the system(s) and the people needing help. This second step involves making a *referral*, which is another way of saying that the worker provides the other system or agency with an appropriate introduction to the person (or group) to be helped. Referrals are sometimes made over the phone or formally by letter. In either method, the worker provides the agency with as much pertinent material about the person and his problem as necessary without violating any confidentiality. Finally, the worker checks that after the system and the person are linked, the problem-solving is accomplished. She does this by maintaining direct communication with both her counterpart at the other agency and with the person with whom she is working. In relation to this, it is important to remember that it is sometimes not sufficient to send an individual to an agency, even if it is the right agency. For various reasons, it is possible that little may be accomplished without the human services worker being present, at least initially. For more effectiveness, the worker should make it her business to go along with her client to solidify her bridge-building with the other system.

Systems are people—in very good disguise. It helps to remember that when one is hesitant to contact a maze of a bureaucracy. It is only counterproductive to conclude that all the people working in a bureaucracy are incompetent "bad guys." (And, even if you do meet a few who are, it won't bring any helpful results to treat them as such.)

Just as it's expected for the human services worker to be able to work respectfully with all individuals, regardless of her personal preferences as to personality types, the same holds true in working with colleagues from other agencies and systems. Mobilizing resources requires that the cooperation of these colleagues be successfully enlisted. Approaching agency workers with respect, openness, and warmth will more likely encourage them to join in the problem-solving than would an attitude of condescension and criticism. In most things, a request is more welcome than a demand and more likely to be met.

The importance of establishing sound, positive professional relationships across subsystems cannot be underscored enough. The old saying, "It's not what you know; it's who you know that counts" happens to be a fact of contemporary life, fair or not. If the human services worker has been able to use herself effectively in developing and maintaining good relationships with her colleagues, her helpfulness is correspondingly increased. Precisely because her work involves systems, it becomes an invaluable asset and time-saver to know a few friendly faces in the bureaucratic crowds who can be relied on to be helpful. Here, too, the human services worker is aware that she should expect to be reciprocally enlisted to help if her colleagues need her services for their clients.

Most of the problems encountered in dealing with systems are not the fault of anyone in particular. Without exception, all the subsystems in the human services were established long ago and are somewhat outdated (if not altogether antiquated) as a result. Another difficulty is that over the course of time the boundaries dividing these systems have become at once more artificial and more rigid. The whole concept of human services spells out the intent to "boundary bust" from now on so that a person and his needs will not be compartmentalized by the subsystems. But, today's human services workers cannot wait for the ideal human services network to begin operating. They must, instead, live and work with the fact that the major theories of human services have not yet been entirely translated into action. Until they are, there will remain fragmented or duplicative services without corresponding, clear linkages to other equally important resources. While the development of an integrated and comprehensive human services network is being completed, workers need to be aware of the existing constraints most likely to impede their problem-solving efforts involving systems:

Fuzzy boundaries • The divisions between the human services subsystems are often unclear, inappropriate, and/or useless. Boundaries tend to decrease the amount of helpfulness available to a person, especially when there are more boundaries than there are linkages. People sometimes "fall between the cracks" of two service empires (i.e., health and mental health; education and child welfare) and never do get the services they need. Or, people can get "locked into" one system and be prevented from deriving the benefits of others (i.e., a man's problems are seen in terms of his health, employment or education only; never in totality). In all her efforts with systems, the human services worker is continually bridge-building and encouraging the development and maintenance of suitable linkages between systems and people, and between systems and other systems.

Communication gaps • Because the subsystems grew up independently, there tended to be minimal communication across subsystems. Sometimes it appears they feel a keen competitiveness to protect their own professional turf. That's one reason why it may appear that subsystems can be at definite cross-purposes. They are often locked in a power struggle. In reviewing the American history of human services development, it was clear that the conflicting values of cooperation and competitiveness were a major obstacle. This conflict is also played out in the subsystems themselves. With the growing acceptance of a multidisciplinary approach to helping, however, it is beginning to seem that more communication will necessarily take place and, hopefully, a substantial increase in cooperation across subsystems will occur. The human services worker takes responsibility for keeping her channels of communication open with other subsystems.

Limited Opportunities • Good linkages and open communication channels between systems are not always enough. Limited resources of systems may become an obstacle to helping. For example, if a worker wishes to refer someone to an outstanding therapy group across town, she may be unable to do so because the hospital sponsoring the group will only serve patients in a certain circumscribed geographic area. Such resource limitations do exist, and it is predictable that they will increase with the continuing growth throughout the human services. The solution to the limited opportunity constraint is not simple and will require sensitive planning. However, in some areas it may be possible for various systems to join forces and merge some of their manpower or other resources. Taking the above example, it may be possible for the human services worker to establish a therapy group in her agency's community, and enlist the hospital's cooperation in providing training and consultation services. Again, the worker's creativity in problem-solving can be the decisive factor in the success or failure of her helping efforts.

Blocked Feedback • In every human endeavor, feedback is vitally important. Without it, we wouldn't know if we were winning or losing, relevant or irrelevant, or even if we were in the right ball-park in all our interactions. This feedback factor plays a vital role in every helping effort by a human services worker. She needs to hear from others whether or not she is being helpful. For the same reason, there needs to be feedback between systems in order that they can measure their helpfulness and modify or enlarge on their procedures accordingly. One source of considerably blocked feedback is the underdeveloped communication existing between rivaling subsystems.

Another source is just as common and usually occurs within a subsystem itself; this is called the *professional distance dilemma*. In the hierarchy that each system supports, it is a fact that as one rises higher on the career ladder, one becomes increasingly removed from contact with the people who come for help. Also, there is a certain amount of foolish arrogance professionals cloak themselves in that separates them even further from understanding the people they are ostensibly trying to help. To compound the damage, as an organization proliferates in size, numerous organizational (i.e., housekeeping) concerns abound that not only detract from helping activities, but sometimes even take higher priority in the administration's mind. All these factors discourage feedback from the consumer—the person being helped. There is sometimes an infuriating "I know best" attitude among professionals and a tendency to do things in traditional ways that are designed to maintain the status quo and to eliminate criticism. Thankfully, the days of those attitudes being tolerated by the consumer are numbered. As consumers increasingly question and demand, the professionals will have to come down from their ivory towers and relearn essential responsiveness to the "whole person's" human needs. Hopefully, feedback between people and systems will then become open. The human services worker, knowing the importance of "People Before Paper" should be a beneficial model for her colleagues as they re-establish priorities.

A WORD ON CHANGE

Working with systems is challenging, though often very difficult for the human services worker. There will be times, to be sure, when the inflexibility and/or injustice of a particular system will invoke rage and a conviction that nothing less than tearing down the entire system or disbanding the whole bureaucracy will do. Well, that usually isn't a rational or feasible idea! Enormous changes made in haste, without sufficient thought about the long-range consequences are, in the end, not only unhelpful, but usually counterproductive. Change, like helping, is a process. It must be planned carefully and rather calmly if it is to bring maximal, positive results.

There are inequities in the systems. Bad things do happen to people because of systems. But, for the human services worker to fly off the handle and denounce the system in its entirety is not going to accomplish much (and none of it good). Even if the worker were to unleash her hostility on a colleague in a system, she might get what she wants that day, but find herself *persona non grata* henceforth and forevermore. In other words, she might win the battle, but she will most definitely lose the war.

Don't take this as an instruction to wear blinders and ignore the flaws and faults in human services systems. It is always important for every worker to be well attuned to the realities of system breakdowns. That knowledge should certainly be put to use in developing strategies for *planful change*. However, the worker is cautioned not to get side-tracked on a crusade which is likely to have negligible or negative results and is going to benefit the person to be helped not at all.

The place for criticisms of system dysfunctions is with your supervisor and among friends who share your professional interests and experiences. With them should begin the kind of discussions and the sifting of information that can lead to planful action and ultimately to constructive change.

BIBLIOGRAPHY

Cartwright, Darwin and Zander, Alvin. *Group Dynamics: Research and Theory.* 3rd ed. New York: Harper and Row, 1968.

Glasser, Paul; Sarri, Rosemary; and Vinter, Robert, eds. *Individual Change Through Small Groups.* New York: The Free Press, 1974.

Kadushin, Alfred. *The Social Work Interview.* New York: Columbia University Press, 1972.

Middleman, Ruth and Goldberg, Gale. *Social Service Delivery.* New York: Columbia University Press, 1974.

chapter nine

———◆●◆———

Social Problems

Your daily newspaper is filled with accounts of the social problems that plague America. Racism, crime, poverty, pollution, family instability, violence, and drug and alcohol addictions are a source of pain for those directly affected by them and a cause for major concern by everyone in the society. Periodically, society becomes interested enough to do something about its problems. A campaign against crime is launched, or more stringent drug legislation is enacted. A war on poverty is declared. Millions of dollars and man-hours are invested in solving the problems "once and for all." Yet, the problems stubbornly persist. Why? Where do our social problems come from? And, why are they so hard to solve?

A society creates its own problems. If society really wants to wipe them out, it is essential that the problems be attacked at their roots. So far our society has not been willing or able to do that. In its most humanitarian moments, there has been a tendency to "throw money at problems" in an almost haphazard way without understanding what caused the problems to grow in the first place. If the human services are to be effective in solving social problems, the underlying forces in society which give rise to its problems must be fully uncovered. Not only should the misery created by social problems be remedied, but also the root causes must be demolished.

THE EMPEROR'S NEW CLOTHES

Hans Christian Andersen, the Danish fairy-tale master once wrote a tale about an arrogant king who insisted on having a magnificent and costly wardrobe. One day, two men approached him and offered to make him a suit of clothes unlike any other in the world. Naturally, in his conceit, he was very interested. The tailors explained that they would weave the cloth of special thread that only people who were extremely wise could see. To everyone else the thread would be invisible. So, when the king did appear in public everyone oohed and ahhed about his magnificent garments (mostly because no one wanted to be thought too stupid to see them). There was a little boy in the crowd, however, who innocently said, "The king is naked." The people began to whisper nervously and then broke into laughter when they realized that the little boy, of course, was right. The foolish king was standing there without a stitch on!

There's a moral to the story that applies not only to human services, but to our society as well. We can easily delude ourselves into thinking that "all is for the best in this, the best of all possible worlds" and that our social problems are neither significant nor cause for much concern. We can go along, blithely believing our own national fairy-tales about "the good life," "equal opportunity" and "social justice." We can choose to believe through the courtesy of the technicolor fairyland of television and movies that everyone has plenty of money, a lovely home in suburbia, "a father who knows best," and a doctor who still makes house calls. We can choose to ignore any feedback which might tell us otherwise and say defensively, "don't confuse me with the facts"!

It certainly is easy to become confused by the facts. Life is complicated enough for those of us who must make ends meet in our own individual lives. There usually is neither time nor inclination to dwell on problems in which we are not immediately involved. People tend instead to rely on "public opinion" as gospel instead of sorting out the confusing and frustrating facts for themselves. As the king's embarrassed subjects found out, however, "public opinion" can often be a distortion of reality and outright inaccurate.

People believe what they want to believe and what they need to believe. That, in large measure, accounts for the popularity of "public opinion" even in the face of its known unreliability. Just as the people in the fairy tale had their own reasons to ignore the emperor's nakedness, so do people in America ignore social problems—they explain them (and explain them away) according to their own personal interests and values.

Social Values vs. Self-Interests

In the earlier discussion of social policy, it became clear that social values play a significant role in setting policy. Those same values also play a significant role in the creation and the understanding of social problems. Here in America we have many conflicting values that stimulate the development of our social problems. Every one of us is motivated primarily by our own self-interests (political, economic, social, occupational, and religious). There is nothing inherently wrong with that. The difficulty arises when we are confronted with some conflict that pits our own interests against those of others. Then we have to decide whether to *compete* or to *cooperate*. Our conflicting urges "to do good" (for others) and "to do well" (financially) will have to be resolved.

Historically, our society has valued competition slightly more highly than cooperation. Our social problems have been the fallout. The value once placed unquestioningly on self-help, individualism, and a commitment to progress for its own sake doesn't make too much sense anymore. Few of us are in line for sainthood and most of us are concerned with protecting our own interests before anybody else's— that's OK. But, are we entitled to protect them at the expense of somebody else's? Is it even possible to act in one's true self-interest without considering the effect on the other guy? Can anyone's self-interest be fully met today without the cooperation of a lot of other people?

President Kennedy once suggested that the time had come in American history to draw up a *Declaration of Interdependence* because the frontier days were long gone and people needed to accept their fundamental interdependence with one another. This is clearly an idea whose time has come. The events in the United States since the Kennedy Administration should help us to realize that, much like in the Emperor's New Clothes, all is not well with our individualistic values or our exclusively self-interested motivations. In the 1970s, an upsurge of unemployment, crime, inflation and incompetent leadership have acted as the boy in the fairy tale to tell us that our complacency about social problems based on a comfortable, large-scale distortion of reality just won't work any more.

BLAMING THE VICTIM

Our social problems may be very widespread and visible now, but they are definitely not twentieth-century creations. They have been around for quite a long time.

To New York City every day come thousands of middle-class and upper-class businessmen, commuting from their comfortable subur-

A suburban home.   *Ghetto homes.*

ban homes. As they approach Manhattan in the morning and leave again at night, they cannot avoid seeing the decaying buildings and the desperation of the slums as they pass by on their trains. I've often wondered how all those reasonably intelligent, usually civic-minded people could see that sight every day and not feel either guilty or angry enough to do something to change it. The reason is that they probably don't see it at all. They are afflicted with *social blindness* (which seems to have reached epidemic proportions!). Just as people believe what they want to believe, they also see what they want to see. And, when they cannot avoid seeing some very ugly realities, they very quickly set out to blame the victim.

Blaming the Victim is a concept developed by William Ryan which explains how society has allowed social problems to thrive under a short-sighted attitude of "benign neglect." The concept is simple: if a person is the victim of a social problem, you simply assume that it's his own fault. All those businessmen on the commuter trains probably took one look at the slums and instantly blamed the victims. They undoubtedly assumed that the people who live in those decaying buildings have chosen to live there and have even chosen poverty because they couldn't be bothered to do better. How convenient! Blame the victim and rest easy.

Blaming the Victim is a concept that is applicable to every social problem now being experienced in this society. It is a convenient way to deal with every incident of inequality and racism, social and economic injustice. It's a simple matter of mixing up cause and effect.

Instead of acknowledging that discrimination still exists many places to keep black people from having equal access to job opportunities, we say that black people are too lazy to look for work. Instead of acknowledging that our tax structure permits the rich to steal from the poor, we claim that the poor "enjoy living that way." Instead of admitting that our teaching techniques are outdated and irrelevant, we blame children for being "hyperactive" or "unmotivated." The possibilities for victim-blaming are limitless.

Blaming the Victim is a method to use when looking for a reason to promote one's self-interests instead of worrying about the other guy. For example, there is no reason poverty should exist in this immensely rich nation of ours. Yet, 11.6 percent of the population is now living in poverty. That's 24,260,000 human beings! Mr. Average American is not heartless and would not consciously elect to send or keep people down. However, if he believes the blaming the victim concept, he can easily relieve his conscience by blaming the victims for their own misfortunes and contentedly assume they could change their lot if they tried hard enough. After all, he argues to himself, this is a free country and people do succeed if they try hard enough. (If he didn't blame the victim, it might mean less of life's good things—in the form of higher taxes, more competition for jobs, etc.) It never occurs to Mr. Average American that people are poor because, by definition, they have no money and because they do not have either the power or the opportunity to make enough money to take them out of poverty. Our society is set up in such a way that it is not possible for the poor to move out of their poverty. That, of course, never occurs to him!

Unfortunately, Mr. Average America isn't always an arch conservative. Many unthinking liberals (including lots of services professionals) are also taken in by the blaming the victim hypothesis—in a word, paternalism. They, too, look at the effects of unjust victim-blaming and see them as causes. Instead of saying that the poor are lazy bums, the liberals will tell us that the poor are living in a "culture of poverty" which keeps them from pursuing the American Dream. Ridiculous! The poor share the same dreams of the good life as the people with money in the bank. The difference is that the poor are cut off from ever seeing such a dream become reality.

Victim-blaming has been particularly effective in justifying the racism that is as characteristic of this country as apple pie. People today frequently wonder how their ancestors could possibly have permitted slavery. That is easy to explain if you victim-blame. All you need to do is say that slaves are less than human and the barbaric treatment that follows is quite all right. This dehumanization process did not end with slavery. Such vicious dehumanizing of other human beings is still going on. We're more sophisticated now and talk about "inferior genes" and such, but the effect is the same. Black people are looked on as somehow less human than others and often treated accordingly. A recent incident of our racial prejudice and victim-blaming towards black people is easily visible in our busing practices. In fact, busing is probably proceeding backwards because of victim-blaming. If society were more objective there would probably be a push to bus the teachers into areas where they're desperately needed—instead of busing the children out!

The existence of poverty and racism are glaring proof that blaming the victim is enjoying wide popularity. Worse than that, we are not only blaming the victim, we are *punishing* him. Out of our own self-interest (short-sighted as it is) we allow poverty and prejudice to continue and then we have the audacity to force the victims to live on the most meager crumbs society will provide. Of course, society is not totally without conscience and has a need to sugarcoat its inequities. So what do we do? We create welfare programs and assorted other well-intended measures to lighten, at least somewhat, the burden of the victims we are punishing. What we don't do is change the tax structure and unfair distribution of wealth that have relegated all those people to the bottom of the social and economic ladder. This is society's way of compromising between its needs "to do good" and "to do well" at the same time. Not a very good compromise, is it?

How do we stop blaming the victim? By doing nothing short of mobilizing for a truly just society, rooted in equitable and comprehensive *income redistribution*. At the present time, 1 percent of the population controls over 40 percent of the nation's wealth. Another 50 percent of the population must share only 25 percent of the wealth. (The gap gets wider as you near the bottom income level.) Clearly, everyone is not getting a fair share of this country's resources. The people with the money are the people with the power and they are not likely to give up either money or power if they can get away with blaming the victim. Certainly effecting a just distribution of income is not going to be a simple task, by any means. But, the first step toward solving any task is reaching an awareness that a problem exists. Acknowledging that we are blaming the victim as an excuse for our own profit motives is a good way to knock the props out from under that outrageous rationalization. It's certainly a good place for everybody in the human services to start!

WAREHOUSING AND OTHER BAND-AIDS

Reflected in society's efforts to deal with social problems seems to be an unfaltering conviction that, "Some people are more equal than others." This assumption is clearly visible in the way society deals with people who have problems. Whatever the problems may be— emotional disturbances, mental retardation, delinquency, alcoholism, drug addiction—society often reacts with the belief that if people have problems, they are somehow inferior beings, less human and, therefore, less equal. Very little thought is given to society's possible role in creating people's problems. Instead of helping people to solve their problems, society decides that the people themselves are the problems. How's that for a tricky variation on the theme of victim-blaming?

Once having blamed the victims for their own problems, society promptly labels them "deviants" and tries to get them out of sight. Under the banner of "helping," society has built thousands of warehouses for its victims and scapegoats. Of course, they aren't called warehouses. They're known as mental hospitals, developmental centers, treatment facilities, and correctional institutions. But, a rose by any other name is still a warehouse.

Who are these "deviants" that society is so eager to push aside? The word itself conjures up images of two-headed monsters or science fiction creatures. Wrong. They are simply *ordinary people with problems*. Some of them can't make it through the day without a drink. Some of them can't read street signs or do simple arithmetic. Some of them can only face life through a heroin haze. Some have the foolish notion that stealing cars is a sensible way to make a living. And, some are just too depressed to get out of bed in the morning. All of them are very unhappy human beings.

It's difficult to understand why society should have such a strong and negative reaction to people with problems. The reason is probably because society's first loyalty is to itself and its primary concern is to protect and perpetuate itself. Society, therefore, seeks to encourage people to conform to its demands. In other words, society wants

Willowbrook institution.

people to be "normal"—hard-working and self-satisfied—in order for the social order to keep running smoothly. When some of the people don't conform and behave in ways that are "abnormal" or "deviant," society feels threatened and feels compelled to ostracize those individuals.

Our society also values strength and self-reliance. When people are troubled and in need of support, their worth is diminished in society's eyes. Society is faced with a peculiar dilemma when confronted by people with problems. On the one hand, society wants to punish them for being different. On the other hand, society wants to help them to feel better. The conflict is resolved by compromise. A meager bit of society's resources is doled out to people with problems and society then feels entitled to forget them with an "out of sight, out of mind" attitude. Traditional efforts to "help" people reflect society's ambivalence about people with problems. Far greater investment has been made in separating and controlling people with problems than has been made in assisting or rehabilitating them. The main thing accomplished in those mammoth, archaic warehouses of the past (usually located far away from the rest of the population) was to give the people with problems more problems than they had before. Now, on top of their original miseries, they were deprived of their liberty and most of their civil rights in the name of rehabilitation and treatment, which were generally fictitious names for custodial care and punishment.

We have only to look at the current data about America's social problems.to see how little those warehouses accomplished!

- **37 percent of all U.S. hospital beds are used for mental patients**
- **9–10 million Americans are alcoholics**

- Over 200,000 Americans are drug addicts
- 1 out of every 6 youngsters will be a juvenile delinquent
- Organized crime reaps over 7 billion dollars annually
- Over 3.5 million Americans are being treated for emotional problems
- The recidivism rate for prisoners stands at 60 percent
- Drugs kill the most people using them between the ages of 15 and 35
- 18.3 percent of all violent crime is committed by juveniles
- At least 1 million children will be abused by their parents this year. Ten times that number will be neglected.

Not a pretty picture.

America has always been in a hurry and often forgets to look before it leaps. This seems to have been precisely the case in our country's attempts to confront and remedy its social problems. Instead of looking at the situation objectively and trying to find out why so many people have so many problems and cause so much misery for themselves and others, there was a rush to remove and punish the deviants, in the hope that the social problems would then be removed as well.

Well, it didn't work! So now we switch from warehouses to band-aids. In the last few years, the atrocities of the warehouses have been exposed as has been the futility of perpetuating them. Throughout the human services the move to *deinstitutionalization* has begun. Finally there is recognition that people with problems need help, not warehousing. People with emotional problems can be served through out-patient facilities. People with a range of health problems, including addictions, can be served by ambulatory care units. People who have broken the law can be rehabilitated through numerous innovations in the corrections field. The focus finally seems to be shifting from the problem to the person, *the whole person*. Certainly that's a giant step in the right direction. Why then is my tone so skeptical?

Unfortunately, society is already showing once again its inclination to "get by on the cheap" regarding its social problems. The warehouses are being emptied, but the alternative services are in frightfully short supply. Society *a)* didn't plan and *b)* didn't pay suffi-

ciently to serve the people new emerging from its warehouses. Those
people still have their problems and still need help. And, society *still*
does not seem to have recognized that the source of its social problems is not necessarily the people who are victimized with problems.
It's really another version of mixing up cause and effect as happens in
victim-blaming. We have concentrated on dealing with the effects of
our social problems and have not given nearly enough attention to
identifying its causes. Our theories of causation are painfully inadequate. For every social problem, the shallowness of our understanding about its cause and cure comes back to haunt us. We need to
start asking some pointed and fundamental questions about our social
problems:

- **What makes people "crazy"? Could the social structure play
  a role?**
- **Why do people turn to crime? Are their other roads to
  achievement blocked?**
- **Why are we ingenious enough to land men on the moon but
  unable to control drug use?**
- **What makes children lawless and violent?**
- **Why do so many millions of people resort to psychic
  crutches, such as alcohol or tranquilizers?**
- **Why do we ignore "white collar crime" and punish severely
  the crimes of the poor?**

These are only a few of the many questions which will have to be
answered if society is to find a way to meaningfully deal with its social
problems. Until those answers are found, it seems unavoidable that we
will continue to apply service band-aids to mortal social wounds. We
will continually apply solutions that are short-sighted and minimally
effective.

FAMILY FADE-OUT

When exactly were "the good old days"? We hear a lot about them,
but I suspect they are really another of our national fairy tales. I'm not
at all sure we should be nostalgic or bemoan the passing of earlier
times. Nor do I believe we should get upset because the American

family has changed right along with the times and isn't what it used to be in "the good old days."

It's true that the family has undergone considerable change during this century. Both the family's typical structure and its main functions are quite different now than they were in grandmother's day. The modern family certainly looks a lot different. The average family size is now no larger than 2.97 members. Only 5 percent of all American families still share their homes with a member of the extended family (such as an aunt or a grandfather). In addition, 43 percent of all married women are now on the working force. The new "nuclear" family is almost a miniature version of grandmother's.

The chief responsibilities assigned to the modern family are also quite different. No longer are the family members required to work together to produce everything they need to survive. Modern families can take life a lot easier with the benefit of a multitude of modern conveniences—from public schools to frozen dinners. Still, the family is charged with responsibilities that are essential to the well-being of the society and everybody in it.

The family must not only devote itself to child-rearing, but must also provide emotional security to all its members and be a source of opportunity through which they can find means of developing their unique potential as individuals. Within the context of the family, every individual is expected to find an avenue for personal growth and meaningful relationships. The family in earlier eras was too busy with other life-supportive activities to give much attention to these areas. Therefore, turning back the clock is not necessarily the answer. However, it is becoming increasingly apparent that the modern family is not well prepared to fulfill these responsibilities either.

The modern family has to be considered a social problem because it is often held accountable for all the other social problems now confronting the confounding the socity. For example, if a child becomes a juvenile delinquent, his family is usually blamed for his behavior. If a woman develops incapacitating neurotic symptoms, her family is usually accused of making life intolerable for her. It is very fashionable in our society to criticize our parents and blame them for our own shortcomings and self-doubts. There are one million runaways every year because of family problems. One out of every three marriages ends in divorce because the family is not satisfying enough. As a consequence, one out of every six families is a single-parent home.

Father and child.

Nevertheless, the family does survive. Most people who divorce eventually remarry. In fact, 97 percent of Americans marry. For all its apparent shortcomings, people still seem to want and need their families. People need roots; they need intimate familial relationships. That's probably why they're still humming, "There's no place like home for the holidays."

The modern family is under tremendous pressure and, at last report, isn't bearing up too well. The family simply cannot make it alone. A number of factors such as increased mobility, peer cultures, the breakdown of neighborhoods, suburban isolation, and inadequate preparation for marriage and parenthood are making it very difficult to maintain a good family life. Add to those factors the problems of job loss or economic insecurity, inadequate housing, and insufficient health, educational, and child-care resources which undermine poorer families and it becomes clear that the American family needs help.

If the family is to be strengthened, society will need to very quickly stop its victim-blaming in this area, too. If families are falling short of meeting their responsibilities, it is not the families who are to be blamed because they buckle under the overwhelming pressures of modern life. Rather, the society must concern itself with either decreasing the pressures or providing the families with an array of supportive services and resources to enable them to withstand the difficulties of modern life.

A good place for society to begin to make amends is at the *poverty line*. In 1976, it was determined that if an urban family of four has an income of under $5,500.00 annually, they are poor. Let's not

even dwell on this ridiculous low figure. Suffice to say that the establishment of the poverty line means that 5.1 million families and 10.2
million children who "qualify" are now living in abject and unnecessary poverty in the richest country in the world! The pressures on
those families to meet responsibilities must be comprehensibly
greater than those their affluent neighbors face. If we really want to
strengthen families, let's begin by raising (or obliterating) the poverty
line and by raising people out of poverty.

In addition to tackling the incongruency of poverty, the human
services must broaden its awareness of the importance of strengthen-
ing and enhancing family life. A commitment to families—to *all*
families—will have to be given high priority. Systems must work for
people so that America's families can be sustained.

SOCIAL SOLUTIONS

America's social problems have so far seemed to be maddeningly
immune to most corrective efforts. This is true largely because we still
have not traced the problems down squarely to their roots. We've put
on "social blinders" as they did in the kingdom of the Emperor's New
Clothes, and we've played the damnable game of Blaming the Victim
instead.

Our traditional solutions to our social problems have failed mis-
erably. The costs, both social and financial, have not been worth it.
The warehouses and the miserly social programs which I call band-
aids have not come anywhere close to solving our social problems or
preventing their proliferation. The old process of social problem solving may have been a costly one and an unsuccessful one, but during
this trial-and-error and wastefulness of human lives and resources, it
is possible that we are finally beginning to understand more accurately what really causes our social problems.

Our mushrooming problems are responsible for finally dealing a
death blow to that outdated frontier ideology: "Every man for himself!" That way of thinking simply doesn't work in this day and age.
The assumption in that credo (that we can all make it, without help, if
we only try) belongs on the shelf with our other national fairy tales.
The attitude isn't appropriate anymore for two reasons. First, *no*body
can really make it very far any more without the cooperation and
support of other people and the society. We are all interdependent,
now more than ever. Second, not everyone has equal access to the

cooperation and support of others in order to adequately meet their needs. Inequality prevents people from sharing equally in the nation's resources and it is inequality that is at the root of our social problems.

Recognizing that inequality is the real culprit, our future efforts to deal effectively with our social problems could well be guided by the principle: When there are social problems, *blame the system, not the victim!* It is not unrealistic to suppose that if society moved swiftly and directly toward eliminating the racial, educational, social, and occupational inequality it now perpetuates, there would soon be a significant decline in our social problems. In the same vein, it is not at all unreasonable to conclude that if society were to provide its families with the services and resources they need in order to function well, it is quite possible that people could live satisfying lives interdependently, free of the label, "social problem."

Inequality and the resulting social problems are generated by the environment. We have already said that if people have problems it means that society's systems are working against them instead of for them. When there are wide-scale social problems it is also because some of society's systems are not working for *all* its people. If the society would minimize its social problems, it must make very sure that its systems are geared towards serving people and that its priorities are people-centered. The task of insuring that systems truly do work for people falls to everyone working in human services.

The society we live in today was planned (if it was planned at all) for the benefit of too few at the expense of too many. We know now that uncontrolled economic growth is leading directly to economic catastrophe. We must also know that insufficient concern about the *quality of life* shared by every individual will lead to human and social catastrophe. The human services planners have set as their goal that every individual in our society should have equal opportunity to meet his economic, social, educational, health and other needs so that he is able to enjoy stable human relationships and to feel some satisfaction in himself and in daily living. To achieve this goal, the human services are concerned now with the prevention of social problems at three levels:

Primary Prevention • eradicating the conditions in society which generate social problems.

Secondary Prevention • assisting the victims of those conditions which generate social problems.

Tertiary Prevention • restoring the victims to fully functioning lives at a level of true equality.

The elimination of social problems requires that a universal
rather than a residual approach must be taken. In other words, the
entire population's needs must be considered, not just those of one
segment of the population. Our earlier social solutions have tended to
be residual in approach and have, therefore, dealt only with some of
the people in the society; i.e., the victims. A universal analysis of
social problems, on the other hand, will use a much broader canvas. To
use William Ryan's words,

> A universalistic analysis will fasten on income distribution as the basic
> cause of poverty, on discrimination and segregation as the basic cause
> of racial inequality, on social stress as the major cause of the majority of
> emotional disturbances. It will focus, not on problem families, but on
> family problems; not on motivation, but on opportunity; not on symp-
> toms, but on causes; not on deficiencies, but on resources; not on
> adjustment, but on change.

The prevention of social problems will be possible only when our
systems really work for people and only when the society makes the
creation of *people-centered social policies* a top national priority.
These people-centered policies would direct the redistribution of society's resources so that the following social goals could be achieved:

- **A full-employment economy**
- **Equitable redistribution of income**
- **Comprehensive health care**
- **Adequate housing**
- **Relevant education**

A commitment to these goals is essential for everybody in our society
and is the foundation of the human services profession.

BIBLIOGRAPHY

Becker, Howard. *The Other Side: Perspectives on Deviance.* Glencoe, Ill.:
The Free Press, 1964.
Duvall, Evelyn M. *Family Development.* 4th ed. Philadelphia: J.B. Lippin-
cott, 1971.

Grier, William H. and Cobbs, Price M. *Black Rage*. New York: Basic Books, 1968.

Harrington, Michael. *The Other America*. Baltimore: Penguin Books, 1968.

Mauss, Armand L. *Social Problems as Social Movements*. Philadelphia: J.B. Lippincott, 1975.

Packard, Vance. *A Nation of Strangers*. New York: David McKay, 1972.

Ryan, William. *Blaming the Victim*. New York: Random House, 1971.

Slater, Philip. *Earthwalk*. New York: Anchor Press/Doubleday, 1974.

Stein, Herman and Cloward, Richard. *Social Perspectives on Behavior*. New York: The Free Press, 1958.

Szasz, Thomas. *Ideology and Insanity*. New York: Doubleday, 1972.

chapter ten

Trends and Issues in
Human Services

In a very real sense this book has been an attempt to explore and explain the trends and issues in human services today. From page one, which posed the questions: "Human Services—What is it? How did it develop? Where is it going?"—the book has tried to present an introductory perspective for understanding what human services is all about and what the human services worker will need to do to enable systems to better serve people. This final chapter will look a little deeper at where human services is going and how it is going to get there. Of course, the future is largely unknown and a dogmatic outline of what's going to happen in our world or in the field of human services would certainly be mostly a waste of paper. Nevertheless, there are clear trends and dominant issues confronting us now in contemporary society with which human services will have to deal if the profession is to carry out its tasks and meet the needs of the whole person and his community.

A city of the future.

NEW PRIORITIES—NEW
DIRECTIONS

"The old order changeth. . . ." It always does! Change is a basic fact of life—it always has been; always will be. Change is not a twentieth-century phenomenon, although the accelerated pace of change may well be. In looking toward the future of human services, we would all do well to accept change as fundamental to the fabric of life today and undoubtedly tomorrow. Throughout history there has been change after change in people's attitudes, needs, and expectations, in their societies and in their social systems, and in their ways of helping one another.

We are told that we're living through an era of *environmental turbulence* and that we're just beginning to feel the side-effects of *future shock*. The implication is that we can outwit the forces of change and somehow manage to capture some peace and quiet, if we can only figure out what's causing all the commotion. That sounds more than a little simple-minded to me. Change just *is* and if we want to maximize the potential of the future, we have to learn to ride the waves, not hold back the tide. We, as individuals and as a profession, have to be prepared for change, to anticipate it, and accommodate ourselves to it.

Though it is usually foolhardy to welcome change for its own sake (like every passing fad), the displacement of old ideas and old ways of doing things is not necessarily a bad thing. Remember that the human services profession emerged because the traditional helping patterns had become too fixed and immobile in their ways of doing things to be able to respond effectively to people's needs today. Even though change creates uncertainty and anxiety, it is also the key to improved service systems and increased satisfactions for people. There is, indeed, a major realignment going on in American society which encompasses our culture and social values, the economy, technology, and the political system. It is a time of anxiety; a time of confusion; a time with no heroes. The days when society's rewards were shared only by Wall Street's empire-builders, Washington's politicos, and Hollywood's fantasy-makers seem to be numbered now. Increasingly, there is evidence of a *new order* and even, perhaps, a new and attainable American Dream—a determination that society's values and priorities should be decidedly more equitable and people-centered than they have ever been before in our history.

Historically, this country has continuously raised the standard of living for its people. Now, there is a growing commitment to enhance the *quality of life* for each of us, as well. This general and widening trend in our society is clearly reflected in a trend for the development of more and better human services. Each of the programmatic trends within human services springs from this major goal—to build a network of human services, committed to personal and family values, to make life more livable for the whole person. Human services is essentially an outgrowth of a renewed societal trend to improve life by *a)* preventing social problems; *b)* reducing the impact of social problems; and *c)* rehabilitating those affected by social problems.

Human services is confronted with a number of issues and challenges related to this societal trend which it embodies. The question must be asked: Are the resources available to human services up to the task? Will there be enough fiscal and manpower resources? Will there be enough information? Will the human services network truly be coordinated? Will there even be enough time? It seems to always have been true that the demand for human services has far exceeded the supply. This will probably continue to be so, given the scarcity which exists in society. However, it becomes the responsibility of the human services to make the best possible and most innovative use of whatever resources are available to minimize the gap between supply and demand. It is not unusual to hear human services professionals claim that they could solve all society's problems and make everyone happy, if only they were given enough money to do it. I doubt it. There's no disputing that there isn't enough money to provide all the human services people could wish for, but that does not mean that the infusion of enormous funds would necessarily guarantee good service delivery either. Human services should not be focusing on becoming more expensive, just better.

The profession, in all its subsystems, is legitimately being challenged about the cost effectiveness of its services. As the general cost of living increases with the times, it is obvious that the cost of delivering human services will also need to increase proportionally. However, we will all be continually challenged (as we should be) to demonstrate that the services we are providing are worth the money. In addition to the twin challenges of proving cost effectiveness and demonstrating responsible accountability, there will also be a need to continue to show that the human services network has relevance and usefulness to the people it is intended to serve.

Human services will seek continually to demonstrate an ongoing commitment to increasing the responsiveness, quality, and performance of systems intended to serve people. To achieve this, the profession must remain flexible and open to change, internally and externally. Human services might well be called a transitional profession for a transitional age. Just as society will continue to evolve, so must human services. Neither will ever be a finished product.

NO TIME FOR AMATEURS

Human services is a profession, manned by professionals. There is a lot of professional skill and competence needed to build a bridge for the whole person that will link him to services. As noted earlier, a solid foundation of knowledge about history, people, society, and resources is fundamental to human services. Good intentions are very honorable, but good management is just as important in human services. Rehumanizing services will be increasingly focused on shaking up traditional patterns of management, time-honored hierarchies and bureaucracies, and unresponsive (or overresponsive) supervisory procedures. Good planning and evaluation in human services will surely underscore the urgent need to develop modern management techniques to improve both the efficiency and effectiveness of every phase of service delivery. Instead of a pyramid model of professional relationships, the active maximum participation of all levels of staff working together should be encouraged. Instead of an autocratic method of decision-making (i.e., by the executive; principal; chief of service; etc.), decisions reached by consensus should be preferred. Furthermore, there should be an open network for expression of ideas and opinions in an effort toward system-spanning cooperation among the disciplines that comprise human services. Modern management should be introduced to effect a refocusing on human needs and community concerns to replace the traditional tendencies to overemphasize the status quo and organizational priorities. In every area of human services, management should stimulate and encourage a willingness to question all factors related to responsive and effective service delivery. Above all, modern management should encourage its personnel to behave humanly and should stress the philosophy of service among equals to replace the professional distance and unequal status that usually exist between the provider and the consumer of human services.

The human services worker's task is formidable. To reiterate, she is expected

- *to relate* to systems and people
- *to activate* problem-solving
- *to integrate* resources and services
- *to evaluate* service delivery

Clearly, this is no job for an amateur. Yet, the human services worker is sometimes, unfortunately and unfairly, looked down on by the rest of the professional community as if she were an amateur. She is even sometimes called a "paraprofessional" or a "nonprofessional" to distinguish (and separate) her from her colleagues with advanced degrees. Rather inappropriately, her credentials are given more weight than her competence. There is a trend in human services to accord more respect and more equal status to the human services worker. This battle is far from won, however. New workers entering the field will have to prove that they, too, are professionals—and valuable ones, even without a string of diplomas and initials after their names. In the English language there seems to be only two choices in occupations: you're either a professional or you're an amateur. In human services today, we have no time for amateurs. And, human services workers certainly are no amateurs.

EVERYBODY'S BALL GAME

Having just said that this is no time for amateurs in human services, let me qualify that statement by saying that there *is* room for the active involvement of the general public throughout the human services subsystems. While it is in no way appropriate to ask or expect a consumer of service to do a professional's job, there is certainly a need for the consumer to be visible and vocal in all areas of human services. In the old days, it was fair game to say, "Caveat emptor" (Let the buyer beware). That is no longer so. The checks-and-balances being built into human services by the active participation of consumers in evaluating services is a healthy new development and a significant trend for the future. Groups such as Nader's Raiders and comparable organizations are performing a vital function in service delivery evaluation. It is too bad that the costs of professional malpractice insurance are rising so fast. However, if this is evidence that more dissatisfied consumers of service are asking for remuneration or compensation for services badly delivered, then it is a good omen for generating better quality services in the future.

There is a concurrent trend in human services which bears attention. This is the remarkable increase in the consumer sector's movement towards self-help groups. Increasingly, previous consumers of service are becoming providers of service. Their effectiveness is generally quite good. For example, groups formed and maintained by alcoholics, abusive parents, widows, and cardiac patients, among others have been able to support and sustain their members in ways which the professional community could not. Are these consumers amateurs? Or, are they professionals? Perhaps, it is to these service providers that the title, "paraprofessional" rightfully belongs. Whatever the title, this type of consumer effort as well as other active roles related to services are hopeful signs for the future.

Contemporary Americans have often been half-jokingly called modern cave dwellers because of the isolation in which they live in their high-rise apartments and their narrow perspectives on the world. The emergence of human services and the increase in consumer input in service development and delivery will hopefully have a positive effect on connecting our cave dwellers more closely to their neighbors and their communities. People, particularly in large urban centers, tend to ignore each other these days. They can no longer afford to do that if we are to share an environment that is not going to become hazardous to our health and well-being. Society is slowly but surely moving towards a realization of people's *interdependence* with one another. Developments in human services will both reflect and promote this ideological shift from overemphasis on an individual's independence from his fellows to his interdependence with them.

It is human services' vision for the future that people will continue to demand an enhancement of the quality of life for themselves and their fellows, and that people will, therefore, demand of the human services uniform and high standards of performance throughout the human services subsystems. It is foreseeable, too, that people will continue to strive for the achievement of a just society in which there is an equitable distribution of wealth and social advantages. The attainment of that goal is a mission to be shared by every provider and every consumer of human service.

A COMMITMENT TO WINDMILLS

Having now come to the end of this piece of work, it's time for reflection. None of this will be easy. The human services are plagued with many save-the-worlders who are either wearing rose-colored glasses or nurturing omnipotent fantasies. There's another group, too—the discouraged ones. There are many professionals who, though committed and skilled, have despaired of helping people because of the inertia of the bureaucracies, the hidden agendas among professionals, the onerous labels pinned on people, and the struggles for turf that go on within and between disciplines. As we've seen, the development of human services has been a series of short-sighted half-measures sometimes and a round of semi-solutions and social blindness at other times. And there has always been the inde-fatigable strength of the status quo to add to the despair. I must confess that rather recently in my career I, too was looking things over and beginning to wonder again what I am doing in this line of work. (It is infinitely easier to sit and write a book than to try to make systems work for people.)

Frankly, I was discouraged. And, you undoubtedly will be too. I started thinking about Cervantes' depiction of poor, noble Don Qui-xote trying to save the world by fighting windmills. That was definitely not an appealling prospect for me. So, I began giving serious thought to doing something very different with my life. But, when all was said and done, it occurred to me that fighting those windmills is not such a bad way to use one's days after all.

How did I come to that remarkable conclusion? Basically, I thought it over and decided that *blaming the system instead of the victim is not enough.* If the system needs changing, then somebody (in cooperation with a lot of other somebodies) will have to change it. Me, included. A few years ago, I was very strongly committed to ending the war in Vietnam. However, when the time came to take a four-hour train ride to march on Washington in protest of the war, I got a little lazy and was reluctant to make the effort. I did finally go and so did thousands of other people. I had figured that my 5'1" frame couldn't make much difference, then I decided that I was wrong. All the heads counted. What if everyone had decided that he wasn't needed?

You and I would probably agree that we want a world in which people share the opportunities and responsibilities in society that go along with freedom, justice, security, comfort, health, growth, and peace—for ourselves, our families, our friends, and our fellow citizens. And, that's why—in spite of all the aggravation and frustration that sometimes comes along with the territory—each one of us needs a commitment to windmills.

Index

A

Acrophobia, 116
Acting, 138–39
Addams, Jane, 50
Advocate, 18
Agoraphobia, 116
American Dream, 38–40
Amnesia, 116
Anxiety reactions, 116
Auctions-in-reverse, 37
Autonomy, 119

B

Belonging, 91
Biological considerations (in
    understanding people),
    107–10
Blocked feedback, 163–64
Broker, 18

C

Calvin, John, 34–35
Care giver, 19
Career ladder, 19–20
Carnegie, Andrew, 42
Childhood and Society, 118
Civil Rights Movement, 61–63
Classes, 111
Claustrophobia, 116
Commonality, 90
Communication gaps, 162
Community planner, 18
Conference of Charities and
        Correction, 50–51
Consultant, 18
Contract system, 37
Conversion reactions, 116
Cultural conditioning, 111
Cultural considerations (in
        understanding people),
        110–14

D

Darwin, Charles, 40
Darwinism, Social, 40–42
Data-gathering in social
    planning, 77–78
Data manager, 19
Depression, 56
Depressive reactions, 117
Diagnostic Center, 82, 83
Direction, 93
Dissociative states, 116

E

Ego integrity, 120
Eight Stages of Man, 118, 119–20
Elizabethan Poor Law of 1601,
    29–30, 33
Erikson, Erik, 118
*Essay on the Principle of
    Population*, 38
Evaluation of social planning,
    79–80
Evaluator, 18

F

Ford, Henry, 54
Free market economy, 38
Freud, Sigmund, 54, 55

G

Generactivity, 120
Goal-setting in social planning,
    77
Groups, working with, 148–56

H

Harris, Thomas, 118
Helping process, 130–44
Helping relationship,
    components of, 96–99
History of human services, 3–6,
    21–45
Hull House, 50
Human services
    definition, 8–10
    goals, 12–13
    philosophy, 10–12
    tasks, 12–13
Hypochondriac, 117
Hysterical behaviors, 116

I

Ideal person, 115
Identity, 119–20
Individuality, 91–92
Indoor relief, 30, 37
Industry, 119
Influence, spheres of, 91
Information and Referral Center,
    82–83
Initiative, 119
Interdisciplinary approach,
    13–20
Intimacy, 120
Issues, 185–94

L

Labels, 114
Laissez-faire, 38, 40
Legislation, reform through, 52

Less Eligibility doctrine, 35
Listening, 135

M

Malthus, Thomas, 38, 41
Manic-depressive reaction, 117
Middle class, rise of, 32
Mobilizer, 19
Modules, 81–85
Muckrakers, 52
Multiservice Center, 82, 83–84
Mutual-aid concept, 31

N

Natural selection, process of, 40
Needs, 212–22
Neurotic, 116
New Deal, 56
New York Society for the
    Prevention of Pauperism, 41
Norms, 111

O

Observing, 136–37
Obsessive/compulsive reactions,
    117
Outdoor relief, 30, 37
Outreach worker, 18

P

Paranoia, 117
Phobias, 116
Planning, social, 75–85

Policy, social, 69–75
Problem identification in social
    planning, 76–77
Problems, 167–84
Productivity, 92–93
Professional distance dilemma,
    163
Program development, 78–79
Progressives, 52
Protestant Ethic, 34, 37, 39, 40
Psychological considerations (in
    understanding people),
    114–21
Psychological era, 55
Psychotic, 117
Puritan Ethic (*see* Protestant
    Ethic)

Q

Questioning, 137–38

R

Reference group, 112
Reform through legislation, 52
Research, 80–81
Residual service, 60
Revolution of Rising
    Expectations, 4–5
Roaring Twenties, 53
Rockefeller, John, 42
Roosevelt, Franklin D., 56

S

Schizophrenia, 117
Self-actualization, 93

Self-awareness, 94–96
Self-esteem, 94–96
Settlement House Movement, 50
Sherman Antitrust Act, 43
Skills, 17–19
Smith, Adam, 38
Social costs, 73
Social Darwinism, 40–42
Social Justice Movement, 52
Social planning, 75–85
Social policy, 69–75
Social roles, 112
Social Security, 52
Social Security Act, 57–58
Social systems, 145–65
Socialization, 110
Society, contemporary, 3–6
Sociological era, 53
Sociopath, 117
Solutions, 181–83
Spencer, Herbert, 40, 41
Statute of 1572, 29
Survival of the fittest, 40
Systems, 145–65

T

Transactional analysis, 118
Transitional Age, 4, 65
Trends, 185–94
Trust, 119
Tycoon times, 42–44

U

Understanding people, 101–23
Universal service, 60

W

War on Poverty, 61–63
Wealth of Nations, 38
Work Ethic (see Protestant Ethic)
Workers in human services,
      16–17
   challenges of, 19
Working with people, 125–44